V:

PF

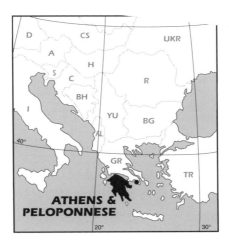

**ATHENS &
PELOPONNESE**

About the Authors

Brian & Eileen Anderson relished the idea of early retirement to pursue their lifelong interests in travel, flowers, photography and history. Brian read botany 2 years full time at Manchester University before they launched into a new career as travel writers. They have spent a number of years living and travelling around the Mediterranean including around 2 years living in various parts of Greece. When at home, they lecture up and down the country on travel and wild flowers.

Acknowledgement

The authors would like to thank the Greek National Tourist Offices in both London and Athens for their tremendous support and help.

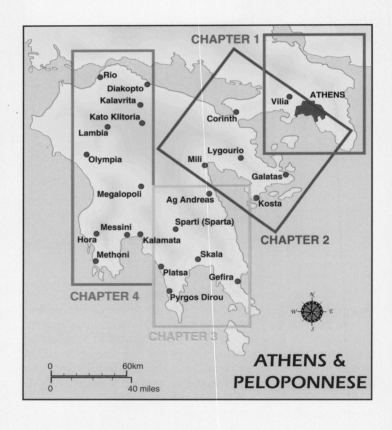

CHAPTER 1

Rio
Diakopto
Kalavrita
Kato Klitoria
Lambia
Olympia
Megalopoli

Corinth

Vilia   ATHENS

Lygourio
Mili
Galatas
Ag Andreas
Kosta

Sparti (Sparta)

CHAPTER 2

Messini
Hora   Kalamata
Methoni
Skala
Platsa   Gefira
Pyrgos Dirou

CHAPTER 4

CHAPTER 3

N
W   E
S

0   60km
0   40 miles

ATHENS &
PELOPONNESE

VISITOR'S GUIDE
ATHENS &
PELOPONNESE

Brian & Eileen Anderson

MPC

<u>HUNTER</u>

Published by:
Moorland Publishing Co Ltd,
Moor Farm Road West, Ashbourne,
Derbyshire DE6 1HD England

Published in the USA by:
Hunter Publishing Inc,
300 Raritan Center Parkway, CN 94, Edison, NJ 08818

ISBN 0 86190 528 8

British Library Cataloguing in Publication Data:
A catalogue record for this book is available from the British Library.

Colour origination by: P. & W. Graphics Pte Ltd, Singapore

Printed in Hong Kong by: Wing King Tong Co Ltd

Cover photograph: Kokkala; Mani (*B. & E. Anderson*)
Rear cover: The Acropolis; Athens (*B. & E. Anderson*)
Page 3: Monemvasia; Laconia (*B. & E. Anderson*)

The illustrations have been supplied by
Brian & Eileen Anderson

MPC Production Team:
Editorial: Tonya Monk
Design: Ashley Emery
Cartography: Alastair Morrison

While every care has been taken to ensure that the information in this
book is as accurate as possible at the time of publication, the publisher
and authors accept no responsibility for any loss, injury or inconvenience sustained by anyone using this book.

CONTENTS

Key to Symbols Used in Text Margin and on Maps

🚶	Recommended walks	⛪	Church/Monastery
🌼	Garden	▦	Building of interest
🏰	Castle/Fortification	⊼	Archaeological site
✳	Other place of interest	🏛	Museum/Art Gallery
⛷	Winter sports	🏞	Beautiful view/Scenery, Natural phenomenon
🦇	Cave		
✈	Airport	🏖	Beaches

Key to Maps

═══════	Multilane Road	·····‹	Nome Boundary
───────	Main Road	─·─·─	Country Boundary
═══════	Minor Road	▬	City
═══════	Unsurfaced Road	○	Town /Village

How To Use This Guide

This MPC Visitor's Guide has been designed to be as easy to use as possible. Each chapter covers a region or itinerary in a natural progression which gives all the background information to help you enjoy your visit. MPC's distinctive margin symbols, the important places printed in bold, and a comprehensive index enable the reader to find the most interesting places to visit with ease.

At the end of each chapter an Additional Information section gives specific details such as addresses and opening times, making this guide a complete sightseeing companion.

At the back of the guide the Fact File, arranged in alphabetical order, gives practical information and useful tips to help you plan your holiday before you go and while you are there.

The maps of each region show the main towns, villages, roads, and places of interest, but are not designed as route maps and motorists should always use a good recommended road atlas.

INTRODUCTION

Greece is full of myths and legends. Every mountain, every rock, every stream and sometimes, it seems, every tree is the subject of some folklore or myth. Nowhere is this more true than in the Peloponnese. It starts with the name: the Greek word Peloponnissos translates into Pelops' Island. Pelops, the son of the mythical Tantalus of Mycenae, was sacrificed by his father and served as a meal for the gods. On discovering this sacrilege the gods were not pleased and devised a suitable punishment for Tantalus. He was left hanging from a tree over water which he could not quite reach and near fruit which forever rustled out of reach on the slightest breeze. He was 'tantalised' this way for an eternity. Pelops fared rather better. Restored to life by the gods he became consort to Zeus and eventually returned to earth as king of the Lydians and Phrygians. He fathered two sons, Atreus and Thyestes, who were rivals in the right to rule Mycena.

The Peloponnese, especially in the Middle Ages, was also known by the name of *Morea*. The mulberry tree figures in most explanations but comparisons to the shape of the leaf are unconvincing. More likely it is a reference to the cultivation of the mulberry tree and the growth of the silk trade.

Although the region is mostly regarded as distinct from mainland Greece with its own discrete character, Pelops' Island is not quite an island. It is a peninsula joined to the northern mainland by a narrow isthmus at Corinth, an isthmus which divides the Gulf of Corinth in the west from the Saronic Gulf in the east. The purists might argue that since the waters of the Corinth canal must be crossed to reach the Peloponnese it is technically an island.

Administratively, the Peloponnese is divided into seven regions or *nomes* with some regions like Corinth and Argolid better known than others. The regional names are often encountered, particularly in accommodation lists.

Its central role in ancient history has left the region with a richness of historical sites second to none in their importance. Mycenae, Ancient Corinth, Epidaurus, Nestor's Palace at Pylos, Olympia are like honey pots to the present day tourists. As fascinating and evocative as these sites are, they are only a part of the Peloponnese and there is so much to discover. Two extraordinary Byzantine towns lie in wait, Mystra in ruins and Monemvasia under restoration. Add to this the castles of Nafplio, Methoni and Koroni, the wild and rugged Mani dotted with tower houses, resorts of character and style like Nafplio and Pylos, the fascinating hill villages of Karitena and Andritsena, the steepest rack and pinion railway in Greece at Kalavrita, scores of monasteries and an inspiring landscape of fierce mountain ranges, lush green valleys and gentle rolling forest and a more complete picture emerges of what lies in store.

Travelling by car is by far the most convenient way of exploring. The roads are mostly surfaced and are generally good with the usual provision that potholes may turn up anywhere, anytime on even the best of roads. Buses from Athens serve the major cities and, within the Peloponnese, each *nome* has a network of local buses radiating out from the main town. Somewhat slower is travelling by train. The Peloponnese is easily able to absorb as much time as you have to spare and still leave you wishing you could stay longer. Two weeks to complete the tours outlined here might leave you just a little breathless while three weeks would feel quite leisurely.

For those who prefer to explore from a resort base, Nafplio and Paleo-Epidauros in the east and Pylos in the south-west have plenty of character but if a good beach is a priority then Tolon near Nafplio and Stoupa in the Outer Mani are worthy of consideration. Those looking for a splendid beach in virtual isolation need look no further than Finikounda.

Most travellers to the Peloponnese start from Athens, that enigmatic city which is the most loved and most fiercely criticised city in Europe. If you put aside the heat, the noisy hum drum of daily life and ignore the mountains of modern concrete, there is a romantic village of antiquity which awaits exploration in the very heart of the modern city. The famed Acropolis, under threat now from modern day pollution, is as evocative as ever despite the cladding of scaffolding necessary for the ceaseless restoration work. Many visitors find time to visit the Acropolis and instantly leave Athens without realising that there is so much more to see. For those bent on discovery, Chapter 1 describes a large number of itineraries, mostly on foot or by public transport, which explore both the ancient and modern faces of this intriguing capital.

People And Culture

It is the conviviality of the people and their hospitality to strangers which makes Greece so special. Unfortunately, these characteristics are seen less in the tourist areas where the Greeks are too hard pressed looking after visitors in great numbers. In all other parts, it takes only a cheerful greeting, sometimes only a smile, to be on the receiving end of their hospitality. It may take the form of an orange pulled from a bag or a handful of freshly grown broad beans but whatever it is, it is considered bad manners to refuse. Language barriers do not exist for the Greeks and mostly they will chatter away in their native tongue in the full expectancy that you will understand some or part of whatever they are saying. Body language and gesticulations play a full part too. The head is frequently used this way. Assent is signified by a slight nod to the side and no is indicated by a slight toss of the head upward often accompanied by a slight 'tchh' sound. If words fail, an invitation to come or to follow is mostly by a downward pawing movement of the hand. If this is an invitation into the home, the first offering will be some sweet preserves served with a glass of water. To refuse this is to refuse their hospitality but it is not essential to eat all of it. No matter how poor the hosts, any suggestion of payment will cause deep offence but a small present for a child would be acceptable. The surprise arrival of a bottle of wine or ouzo on your table in the taverna may well be the gift of a new acquaintance. The custom here is to pour a glass to toast the sender and drink at least a little of the bottle but there will be no expectation that it is all consumed. The penetration of polite conversation often takes visitors by surprise. After the usual health enquiries, which are taken seriously by the Greeks, the conversation quickly moves into questions about the family, how many sons, daughters and their ages. Unreserved admiration is expressed for parents of large families especially with many sons. From this point enquiries continue about work and will invariably contain a question which throws unprepared visitors almost into a state of shock; 'How much do you earn?' In Greek society it would be considered impolite not to ask this question.

The family unit is strong and still the basis of Greek society, although there are signs that the bonds are starting to weaken under western influences. It is sons who receive the adulation and are totally spoilt by their parents. This does not mean that daughters are

Happily watching the world go by is a favourite Greek pastime

*Cheerful locals,
passing the time of day*

A street artist at work

not welcomed, as in some societies, and the ideal family is regarded as one son and one daughter. It is remarkable just how many Greek families comprise just two children. In reality they have been using abortion as a means of birth control for a long time. Parental influence is still strong when the time is right for their children to marry. Arranged marriages have not entirely disappeared but they are no longer the norm although parents still have a dominant role in satisfying the demands of society and tradition. It is the duty of the son to stand by his parents to ensure that suitable matches are made for all his sisters before he can contemplate marriage. Although a dowry is no longer a legal requirement, and this repeal was only in recent times, it is still perpetuated. A girl goes into marriage with the gift of a furnished house or apartment from her parents. It remains the girls property and her security. In the same way gifts of gold to the bride are not unusual. The parents have a working lifetime to prepare for providing a home for their daughter or daughters but, such is the pressure from society, failure to succeed may mean that they have to relinquish their own home when the time arrives. At least the newly wedded couple start life without the burden of debt and are able to build and plan a future for their own children. The family unit extends into business too. The Greek preference is for self employment, failing that a secure job with the state, and most of the small businesses employ only family which are eventually passed down via sons and daughters.

It is a male dominated society in which it is demeaning for a man to indulge in women's tasks. This distinct role division is ingrained into society and a woman would lose face if her man was seen sweeping floors or washing dishes. Attitudes are slowly changing amongst the younger generation. The segregation of the sexes too is inbuilt into society. When family or friends enjoy a meal in a taverna, which can be quite a boisterous affair, there is usually a polarisation where the men cluster to one end of the table and the women to the other. Only young men have the freedom to go out alone and it is not uncommon to see them dining out in groups but mostly they head for the bars and congregate there in large numbers. Again signs of change are evident even in this area. The role of the women in the broader society has been recognised in legislation. They acquired the vote only in 1952 and the first woman Deputy was elected to Parliament the following year. Sexual discrimination in career opportunities and in the place of work has been outlawed. Many practical steps have been taken to assist the integration of women as equals in society. Low cost nurseries providing child places have been provided to free women to work and they have acquired rights of ownership after marriage and an equal share of communal property on divorce. Women now hold important posts in all branches of the Civil Service and in commerce but, in spite of all their progress, equality is only accepted in the big cities. Throughout rural Greece it remains contrary to the culture and fundamental change will only be fully accepted very slowly. For women travelling alone in Greece there are no exceptional problems. The incidence of violent crime, including rape, is much lower than in other western societies. But it is not unknown and the same wariness of the possible situations should be observed. Greek men firmly believe that they are irresistible to all women so their attentions can be expected. Women alone in bars or tavernas may cause some raised eyebrows but they will be served without question.

Geography And Topography

Occupying the southern tip of the Balkan peninsula, Greece is firmly located in Europe. With a land area estimated at 131,944sq km (51,540sq miles) and only around 10 million people it approximates to a population density of 76 people/sq km (200 people/sq mile). That assumes an even spread but it is not evenly spread. Since some 4 million people alone live in Athens or its immediate surrounds this leaves many of the other areas very thinly populated.

Geographically the mainland is divided into seven regions and each of these is further divided into administrative units known as *nomes* (*nomoi*), making a total of thirty-nine. Excluded from these is the monastic republic of Mount Athos which has its own administration. Each *nome* has a chief town regarded as the capital which often also serves as the hub of the regional bus service. The visitor is perhaps most aware of the existence of *nomes* in the Peloponnese where Arcadia and Argolid are already familiar names. Pick up any accommodation list in Greece and it is almost certain to be subdivided under *nomes*.

In the Peloponnese, there are a number of ranges of which the Taygetos, in the southern part running down into Mani, is the best known. Just to the north-west lies the Parnes which runs almost parallel and in the north is a cluster of ranges which includes the Aroania and Mount Helmos. There are many peaks over 2,000m (6,560ft) with the highest mountain Profitis Ilias peaking at 2,407m (7,895ft). Winter snow which covers the tops of all these mountain ranges persists throughout the spring months into early summer. There may be permanent snow patches in the hollows around the mountain tops but there are no glaciers. With such high mountains and so much snow around, it might be expected that there would be many fast flowing rivers. In fact there are relatively few rivers and none of them navigable. There are plenty of dry river beds around which take away the flash floods from the winter storms and are almost instantly dry again.

Politics

Politics is an overriding obsession with the Greeks. Free political expression arrived only in 1974 with the fall of the dictatorship. All the three hundred seats in the single chamber parliament are filled by parties formed after 1974. Essentially a two party system is evolving with the contestants being the socialist PASOK, the Panhellenic Socialist Movement and the New Democracy party (ND) with conservative leanings. Not without some support is the Communist Party of Greece, the KKE. All these symbols are liberally painted on bridges and buildings throughout the country. After years of socialist rule, the New Democracy under Mitsotakis held power for a time before elections in 1993 returned a Socialist Government again. The political system is slowly maturing but it still faces some serious problems in bureaucracy, nepotism, petty corruption, low productivity and poor social services. Greece's membership of the EEC has itself been a stabilising influence and the country has benefited greatly from grants, enormous loans and subsidies over recent years. A stabilisation programme imposed from Brussels is currently in place trying to reduce government spending and bring inflation under control. Regardless of which party holds the balance of power, strikes are a way of life in Greece and barely a week passes without some sector providing the action. It does occasionally become a serious problem for the traveller when the action moves into a concerted phase and banks, transport and tavernas, for example, all co-ordinate their strikes.

Economy

Traditionally, Greece's economy was based on farming and small scale manufacturing but there has been considerable change over recent years. After the war years, up to around 1970, about half the labour force worked on the land and agricultural products contributed significantly to the countries exports, as they still do. Unimpressed with the hard life and poor returns, the younger generation started to move to the cities and to the developing tourist centres for better paid work. The exodus seriously depopulated some areas, like the hill villages, where farming was nothing more than an existence.

Since joining the EEC in 1981, the farming sector has benefited considerably from subsidies and has enjoyed a considerable improvement in its standard of living. Shipping and tourism are two of the major stabilising factors in the Greek economy, both big earners of foreign currency. With so much coastline and the sea offering easier travel than the mountainous interior, Greece has had a strong shipping sector from ancient times. With troubled times for too many years this century and with unfavourable government policies, many of the shipping magnets had registered ships under a flag of convenience and moved their centre of operations away from Greece. All that has changed in the last few years under the influence of revised government policies. Many have returned to the Greek flag and maritime earnings have steadily increased. Currently, Greece has the largest merchant fleet in the EEC and the fifth largest in the world. There is a view that if all Greek ships were Greek registered then it would have the largest fleet in the world. Piraeus, close to Athens is the countries biggest port and this is in the throes of a modernisation plan to improve facilities and handling for shippers. Other major ports include Volos, Igoumenitsa, more important following closure of the land route to Europe through former Yugoslavia, Thessaloniki and Patra.

A colourful fishing boat moored at Paleo Epidauros harbour

Tourism is a more recent success story. Boasting 3,000 hours of sunshine a year, a host of beautiful islands and a wealth of historical interest, it has succeeded almost in spite of itself. It is generally acknowledged that there are more things wrong in Greek tourism than right. Unlike other nations which have perhaps tried harder, the Greeks have not gone overboard building water-chutes, theme parks and all the other features regarded as desirable. Unwittingly, they may have found the key to the successful development of tourism. Tourist resorts in Greece are as near natural as any in the Mediterranean and their lack of sophistication and the natural charm of the people are important elements which attract visitors back and back again. Infrastructure improvements in terms of new roads, water supplies and better support services are in hand which the government hope will promote new developments in the quality sector. At the moment the season is limited to the main summer months and the longer term strategy is to develop all year round tourism.

The third major source of foreign income is from the remittances sent home by the emigrants. For a period after World War II and civil war which followed, when the country was truly devastated and the prospects for employment very poor, there was a period of mass emigration in which many thousands of Greek men and their families departed overseas, mainly to Australia but also to America and Africa. It is often jokingly said that if all the expatriates returned home the population would double. The Greeks seem to work harder abroad and many proved successful in business enterprises. They did and still do send money home to support their parents and brothers and sisters although there has been something of a drift back in recent years, especially in retirement.

To complete the economic picture, the country still has little manufacturing capacity and its main exports are in fruit and vegetables, wine, tobacco, textiles and jewellery.

Law And Order

The incidence of violent crime, theft and robbery is still far lower than in most other western cultures, although there are signs that it is on the increase in Athens. It is not something that need concern the tourist and to be able to move around in the evening without feeling threatened in any way is one of the pleasures of this country. It still pays to be sensible with personal property and protect it as at home. Generally, the Greeks have their own moral code for living in which there are some distinctly eastern traits and ambiguities. They have a basic honesty which means that if you leave your change in their shop then they will chase down the street after you to return it. On the other hand, the same owner may well have twisted you out of a few *drachmas* by quoting a wrong price. This is regarded as smart and foreigners are fair game.

Religion

The Greek Orthodox Church is firmly established and dominates the religious scene. Other denominations are tolerated but proselytisation is not. The Archbishop of Athens and All Greece heads the church which is governed by a synod of the bishops and other leading members. Some of the church's income arises from the state but more from its massive real estate interests acquired in earlier years. Priests move about the community in their black ankle-length cassocks, black hat and full beard. They may be seen drinking coffee in the kafeneon and travelling by bus when, more than likely, someone will spring up to offer a seat but they are rigidly church based without the role of social worker in the wider community. As in many other western cultures, the church is slowly losing its power amongst the people, especially the younger generation. The acceptance of civil marriage was forced on the church by the government following reforms in 1981. Up until that time, Greeks married abroad by civil ceremony were not accepted as married under the Government's own civil law. Abortion too was legalised, also against church opposition, but this did nothing more than legalise the existing high rate of abortion. It has long been used as a means of family planning and remains, even now, the most widely practised form. Other forms are still very much under the counter. The Church still controls a lot of agricultural land and unused land which the government is trying to wrestle away to put into the hands of farmers and cooperatives.

On high days and holy days, and there are many in the Greek calendar, the church comes into its own and, for a brief time becomes the focus of community life. Easter is the most important event of the year and this and other religious events are discussed in the Fact File. The church played an important role throughout the Byzantine years as guardian of the Greek culture. It organised secret schools to educate the children and preserve the language.

Food And Drink

Eating out in Greece, traditionally inexpensive, is a national pastime but even that is under threat with rising prices and high rates of inflation. It was unthinkable for a Greek family to entertain friends or family to a meal at home. As a party they would head for the taverna and the host would collect the bill. Not only was the taverna a place to eat but it was also a place of entertainment. After the meal, tables would be pushed back, the owner would produce a bouzouki or similar instrument and the menfolk would rise to dance. Perhaps later the women might join the dancing too. Sadly this now happens only on festive occasions. Gone is the bouzouki to be replaced by the television and the atmosphere of the taverna is generally more subdued. Watching the Greeks eat is a pleasure in itself. Seldom do they order individually, instead they order a vast number of communal dishes which fill the table to overflowing. There is no rush to eat the food either, conversation continues at a high pitch whilst the diners pick and nibble their way steadily through the dishes. They are far less concerned about cold food and many dishes which arrive hot are cold before they are eaten. Some tourists find it a bit disconcerting when their meals are actually served on the cool side but, in most tourist areas, the message that tourists generally like their food hot has registered.

Although the Greek cuisine is quite extensive, tavernas tend only to have a limited menu. Lunch time, between 2 and 3pm after work finishes, is the only meal of the day for which the chef will prepare a range of cooked dishes. For the evening trade, and the Greeks are notoriously late eaters, the menu offers whatever is left over from lunch, which has often been kept warm for hours, and a range of grills which are cooked to order. Charcoal is generally used for grilling and it is not unusual to see large charcoal grills by the doorway or outside in summer. Although the tavernas are the traditional eating places, cities and larger towns may also have restaurants which provide a better standard of decor in particular and tend to have a more international cuisine.

Tavernas are obliged to have a menu but many still do not. Instead diners will be shown a glass show case exhibiting the range of dishes available or, and this is still very common in the villages, they will be led into the kitchen to see exactly what is cooking. If difficulties are experienced in the final choice then spoons may appear for a tasting session. In an effort to improve standards, there has been a recent government decree instructing that all tables should have a cloth table cloth. Previously it was usual just to have a plain piece of polythene which was changed for each new client. It served a double purpose because at the end of the meal all scraps from the plates would be tipped into it and the whole lot bundled up and removed. Now the situation has changed. Tables are fitted with a decorative

The Swallowtail Butterfly (Papilio machaon), *is one of the best known species in Europe and fairly widespread throughout Greece*

Greece, one of the most floristically rich areas of Europe; Iris Attica

table cloth but this is securely protected by a polythene sheet covered by a paper square and only the latter is laid fresh each time. Should there be a menu on the table then it will probably be in Greek and English but it will only show a partial correspondence with the dishes on offer so it still pays to ask. It is unusual to find the table laid, apart from the oil and vinegar flasks, paper napkins and the inevitable toothpicks, but the cutlery arrives with bread after an order is placed.

There is no special form in a taverna and no conventions to follow. The Greeks often go in for a plate of chips and a beer and make it last half the night. For diners though, it is usual to begin with one or a selection of the starters or *mezedes* on offer. These include *tzatsiki* (a yoghurt, cucumber and garlic dip), *taramasalata* (fish roe mixed with potato, oil and vinegar, the pinker the better), *melitzano salata* (an aubergine dip with tomato and garlic) and *humus*, another dip this time from chick-peas. Fresh vegetables are rarely available but two vegetables which turn up as *mezedes* are *gigantes* (butter beans cooked in tomato and oil) and peas (*arakas*). *Saganaki*, fried cheese is another interesting starter. The waiter will raise an eyebrow if *mezedes* are ordered separately by each individual, even tourists are expected to order a selection and share in Greek style. Salads may be preferred as starters or as part of the starters and the most popular is the village salad or *horiatiki salata*. The content of this mixed salad is laid down by regulations and it should include lettuce, or cabbage, tomato, onion, cucumber, a certain weight of feta cheese and olives. A few years ago, a salad like this constituted a meal in itself and many tourists were perfectly happy to make a lunch from it. Unfortunately, this made the taverna owner less than happy, consequently the price has risen considerably and they are not always the generous portions they were. Tomatoes, cucumbers, feta cheese and lettuce (*maruli*) are all offered as separate dishes. Ready cooked dishes may include the familiar *moussaka*, a mince dish with aubergines, potato and bechamel sauce, veal in tomato, *stifado* (veal stew with onions) or *giovetsi* (oven cooked lamb served with pasta). Chicken cooked on the spit is popular and an inexpensive dish but favoured amongst the grills is *souvlaki*, veal or pork on a skewer. Chops, pork, lamb or veal, are ever present on the evening menus as are *keftedes* (spicy meat balls) and *biftekia* (mince burgers). Fish is sometimes on offer but for a selection it is better to find a fish (*psaria*) taverna. Lobster (*astakos*) and red mullet (*barbounia*) are usually top of the menu and are expensive as are shrimps (*garides*). Octopus, grilled or cooked in wine is less expensive as is squid (*kalamari*). At the cheap end is the small whitebait (*marides*) which is eaten in its entirety, head and all.

This dish is often available as a starter in a fish restaurant. Trout is sometimes on the menu in mountain areas. Desserts are very limited, usually fruit, but the popularity of yoghurt and honey amongst the tourists is now recognised. If you have tucked into your meal with obvious enjoyment, the proprietor may produce a plate of fruit, peeled and presented with his compliments.

Some Greeks prefer to drink ouzo with meals and this is served in small bottles and usually taken with water. Others choose *retsina*, a resinated wine, which is an acquired taste. Often the *retsina* is from the barrel and locally made. Some of this can be very good, especially if lightly resinated, and it is worth trying a glass to start with. It is more than likely that the wine list will contain some good wines like *Boutari*, *Naoussa* and *Lac des Roches* as well as some medium priced popular wines like *Kambas* and *Rotonda*. Labels such as these are generally available throughout the country but there are a large number of branded local wines which are equally good. Many Greeks themselves have vines on their own farms and it is worth asking for *krasi dopio* (wine of the house), which at least is cheap and can vary from excellent to undrinkable but is usually exciting enough to risk the experiment. In most regions there is a locally made unbranded wine and this too is worth a try although some of it might be lightly resinated.

Flora And Fauna

Greece is one of the most floristically rich areas of Europe and boasts over 6,500 species. The Peloponnese has its fair share but it is the April visitor who will see them at their best in the lowland areas. For those happy to climb mountains, June and July are good months for finding flowers.

The lowlands enjoy a Mediterranean climate, hot dry summers and cool, moist winters making winter the favoured season for plant growth and summer a time for resting, at least for the shallow rooted plants. Plants with underground storage organs, like bulbs, corms and rhizomes revel and are profuse throughout the Peloponnese. Flowers which catch the eye and can be found everywhere include anemones, muscari and wild orchids of which there are many. Annuals too, which survive the summer as seed, are abundant and often provide colourful displays in spring.

In the mountains the climate is different with temperatures in winter too low to sustain plant growth but with plenty of sunshine and rain in summer. The flora here is more typical of that seen in Europe. Crocus, hellebores and saxifrages are just a few of the species which thrive in these habitats.

A number of small mammals are around including the red squirrel, frequently seen amongst the pines, rabbits and foxes. The larger mammals are confined to isolated mountain regions where wolves, wild goats, chamois and wild boar still survive although some on the edge of extinction. Bird life is plentiful, especially with the smaller species (swift, swallow, chaffinch and goldfinch) but for wetland species including purple herons and little egrets, the Marathon marshes near Athens are worth a visit.

History

Historical Greece, long regarded as the cradle of civilisation, attracts archaeologists, historians and researchers as nowhere else on earth. Already the knowledge and understanding of historical events in this part of the world is enough to fill volumes and it continues to grow. This brief account aims at nothing more ambitious than to lend some perspective to your travels. In this respect it will concentrate largely on events on the mainland and dwell more on the age when the great temples and cities were built. Nowhere else in the world does the force of history overwhelm the mind in such a startling fashion as when you are standing amongst rocks fashioned and placed by the hand of man with such architectural brilliance. It is sometimes necessary to pinch yourself to remember that they were built millenniums of years ago.

Early history is conveniently divided into periods. Convenient in that, once recognised, they provide a time scale reference which is easier than remembering individual dates. These key periods are:

3000BC-1100BC	(Bronze Age)
1100BC-800BC	(Dark Age)
776BC-480BC	(Archaic Period)
480BC-338BC	(Classical Period)
338BC-146BC	(Hellenistic Period)

BRONZE AGE (3000BC-1100BC)
A significant point to start the story is with the development of two great civilisations within the Bronze Age. The first to crystallise was the Minoan civilisation on Crete around 2200BC. It was a remarkable, structured culture which built palaces, developed religion, traded by sea throughout the Mediterranean and developed art and pottery to a degree of sophistication not seen before. Historians have learnt much about the culture from the wall frescos depicting scenes of daily life and from the decorated, elegant pottery. The Minoan

civilisation showed many stages of advancement over the long period of its history. Natural disasters were believed to have hastened the decline of this civilisation, especially the massive volcanic eruption on Thira (Santorini) around 1450BC.

Greece at this stage of its history did not exist as a single nation nor did it conform to the political boundaries as they are now understood. There existed a large number of independent tribes occupying, not just the lower part of the Balkan Peninsula, but many parts of the Mediterranean including settlements on the Black Sea. It was easier to trade and communicate using the seas than the mainland. On the mainland, tribes were isolated by the mountainous terrain and the difficulty of travel. They shared common features of which the most important was language; they all spoke the Greek language or a recognisable dialogue. People who did not speak Greek were thought to make noises which sounded like bar-bar and were referred to as *barbaroi* (barbarians).

The second great civilisation formed in the Peloponnese, around Mycenae, and soon dominated southern Greece. The culture grew slowly from an early date with the migration of Indo-Europeans down from the Balkans and rose to dominance from 1600BC to 1100BC. Much of its art was influenced by the Mycenaean culture on Crete and possibly its life-style too. It was not until the destruction and decline of the Minoans that the Mycenaeans had their chance to develop trade throughout the Mediterranean which they soon came to dominate. At the height of their power, they had constructed some 320 citadels throughout mainland Greece and the Aegean. Today the most important of the ruins associated with the Mycenaean cultures are found at Mycenae, Argos, Tiryns and Nestor's Palace at Pylos.

It was an ordered society ruled by a King who was also chief priest and supreme judge supported by an aristocracy and a warrior class. Evidence for this comes from the royal graves. These were magnificent circular domed tombs a few of which were discovered unplundered. They yielded bronze weapons and gold, gold in the form of diadems, cups and funeral masks.

The Mycenaean culture had certain strong characteristics most evident in its architecture. They built simple, austere stately palaces which were strongly fortified by enclosing walls built in massive masonry and sited for defence. It was an autocratic rule which relied on wisdom and strong leadership from the King who used his knowledge of astronomy to set the calendar for all the important events of the year from religious festivals to cycles of nature, when to sow and when to harvest. Knowledge of the history of this period was gleaned from the artefacts from excavation, from epic poetry and history written at a later time and from Linear B script which was interpreted finally in 1952. The Mycenaean age was an age rich in folklore, in heroes, personalities and events which are captured and encapsulated for posterity in the works of Homer, especially *The Iliad*. Agamemnon was a giant amongst the personalities of that time. King of Argos, he led his warriors to besiege Troy in revenge for the abduction of Helen, his sister-in-law and the most beautiful woman in the world.

The reasons for the eventual decline of the Mycenaeans are not entirely clear. One by one the citadels were sacked and burnt but whether by internal revolution or invasion remains unresolved. The Dorians moving down from the north with superior weapons of iron are believed to have some influence. Slowly, as the autocratic structure of society crumbled, Greece entered a new period known as the Dark Age.

THE DARK AGE (1100BC-800BC)

The label Dark Ages is often used to disguise the fact that little is known about a period. This period spanning 300 years falls into that category. It was one of chaos and transition. Greek speaking Dorians from the north moved down to occupy the whole of now mainland Greece including the Peloponnese. It was a merging of tribes rather than an annihilation of some. Artistic and material advancement ground to a halt but slowly a new vision of political and social organisation emerged.

THE ARCHAIC PERIOD (776BC-480BC)

The rapid spread of the Phoenician alphabet across the Mediterranean marked the beginning a new phase. A phase which re-appraised the basis of society and laid foundations for the growth and development of city-states.

It was an energetic period throughout. Written records started which gave the first reliable insight into early history. The works of Homer, thought not to be the works of one man, were written down by 750BC and around the same period Hesiod formalised Greek mythology. New levels of artistic expression surpassing those of the Mycenaean period are observed in the many artefacts from this period including the monumental work. Architecture did not quite match the pace of advancement but new materials and principles were being explored which were to flourish in the Classical Period.

City-states developed to replace the old autocratic rule. The leaders were usually aristocratic warriors but they ruled by consensus in an early form of democracy. Public debate was encouraged and inscribed codes of law started to appear. Cities (*polis*) differed in construction too. Usually a defendable position like a hill top (*acropolis*) was still favoured but the palace structure of the Mycenaean period was now replaced by a temple to the gods of the city and life revolved around the market place (*agora*) where public debate and business took place. Various city-states started to associate to form regional power bases raising cities like Sparta in the Peloponnese and Athens to greater prominence.

Stone replaced wood as the material for building columns leading to the appearance of Doric columns in the Peloponnese (around 650BC) and Ionic columns in eastern Greece (around 600BC). Philosophy too had its roots in this period. With new found freedom of expression, thinkers started to reflect on the new political order and the effect on the individual. Over in the east the Persians had begun to expand their empire towards the Mediterranean which was soon to threaten Greece.

THE CLASSICAL PERIOD (480BC-338BC)
Classical as a term is now widely used to describe ancient Greek history in general but historians adhere steadfastly to the narrower definition.

The epic battles of the Persian wars are well chronicled. Leading his army against Athens, Darius failed when his fleet floundered on Mount Athos as he tried to round the peninsula. Two years later (490BC), after rebuilding his fleet, he sailed directly across the Aegean to land at Marathon, 42km (26 miles) north-east of Athens. The Athenians left the safety of their city to carry the attack to the Persians before they had time to deploy their superior military force on land. Athens won a famous victory and Phidippides, running with the news back to Athens only to die on reaching the stadium, became a legend. Darius died in 486BC leaving his son Xerxes to continue the fight against the Greeks. With renewed determination, he raised a massive force and entered Greece to fight the battle of Thermopylae in 480BC. An heroic force lead by Leonidas, the Spartan King, delayed the advance of the Persians at the cost of their lives. The Athenians evacuated their city to regroup at Salamis where the more manoeuvrable ships of the Greeks crushed the superior Persian fleet. The Persian army returned to capture and sack Athens in that same year. One year later, the Persians were finally annihilated by a combined army of Athenians, Spartans and other allied city-states.

The end of the war against the Persians marks the start of the Classical Period, a new golden age which saw the rise of Athens and a considerable advance in political and cultural achievements. More than 200 city-states joined the league of Delos to contribute money to a defence fund which was used to liberate the eastern Greek cities in Asia. Pericles used the remains of the fund for a lavish rebuilding programme of Athens, the Acropolis, the Parthenon and the whole complex. It became a period of temple building throughout the region using new mathematical skills to introduce subtleties into the design to enrich the harmonious appearance. Drama advanced and theatres were built using the natural contours of the land. Art and sculpture too evolved and reached new levels of attainment and it was in this period that Pheidas sculptured the Parthenon marbles. Columns of the Corinthian order which use the acanthus leaf decoration at the capital were first used about 450BC. The temple of Apollo at Bassae is an early example.

The outlines of democracy which had emerged earlier were formalised and further developed. A code of law was established in Athens. Power was exercised initially by representatives from important families but this evolved into a council of 500 drawn by lots from neighbouring tribes. Pericles remained an important figure and retained power for almost 30 years.

Sparta and Athens remained in competition with each trying to

Removals by donkey are a speciality in Greece!

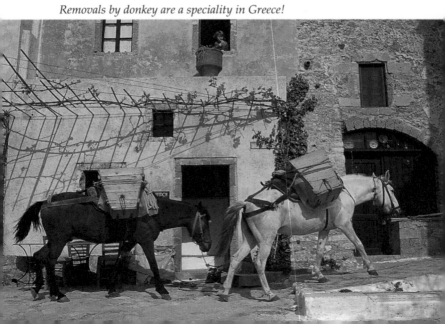

expand its power. While Athens formed the Delian League based on the sacred island of Delos, Sparta established the Peloponnesian League which included mainland cities such as Delphi. Skirmishes between Athens and Sparta which started in 457BC developed into a full scale war in 430BC. Sparta emerged the eventual winner at the close of the fifth century. Athens lost imperial power but soon regained much of its influence.

The second part of the Classical Period is characterised by a gradual unification of the city-states under the power and leadership of King Philip II but not without some resistance on the way. Against slow but profound political changes of the fourth century, the influence of philosophers made their own impact. Plato and Aristotle started their own schools and Plato's Academy in Athens could lay claim to being the world's first university.

In 338BC, King Philip of Macedonia won a decisive battle which saw the final unification of the city-states and marked the end of the Classical Period.

HELLENISTIC PERIOD (338BC-146BC)

The assassination of King Philip in 338BC brought the young, 18-year-old, Alexander to power and started a new phase in Greek history. Already blooded in battle and with great powers of leadership, he took the fight right into the enemies camp, the Persians. The first task was to liberate the Greek colonies in Ionia and from there he continued to sweep through Asia. He had the wisdom not to sack the cities but to preserve and enslave the people. Under his leadership, the Greek Empire spread rapidly and soon extended as far as India in the east and Egypt in the south. Alexander died in 323BC at the age of 32 and is remembered as Alexander the Great. Proclaimed a god by the Egyptians, he founded his own city, Alexandria, which eventually replaced Athens as the centre of Greek culture. Throughout his massive Empire he spread Greek art, literature and philosophy and scholarship which were to have their influence through the following centuries.

After his death, the kingdom was divided into territories ruled by generals but the system was too loose to survive very long and the political structure soon dissolved. Away to the west, the Romans were gradually increasing their power and by 200BC Rome was in control of the city-states of the Italian peninsula. Over the next 50 years Rome steadily increased its influence over Greece.

THE ROMAN DOMINATION (146BC-AD330)

Attacks by the Greeks on the Roman envoys in Corinth in 146BC proved to be a significant event. The Roman army descended on Corinth and completely destroyed it and continued to establish control over the whole Greek Empire. They abolished democracy and substituted their own military control making Greece nothing more than a province of Rome. This marked the end of independent ancient Greek history. As far as the traveller is concerned, the other significant period in Greek history which is still present through its architecture is that of Byzantine and medieval times stretching from AD395 through until the Turkish occupation in 1453.

In the decline of the Roman Empire, Constantine became the emperor in control of both east and west. The site he chose for a new capital was Byzantium on the Bosphorus which was originally founded by Byzas in 630BC. From Byzantium emerged the new spiritual and political capital of the Byzantine Empire, *Constantinople*, which was to hold power for almost a thousand years until its ultimate collapse in 1453.

Constantine died in AD337 and was baptised a Christian on his deathbed but it was not until AD380 that Christianity became the state religion. Shortly afterwards a proclamation was made to close the heathen temples like Delphi and the Parthenon. Even the Olympic Games were discontinued because of the nudity. Temples were now converted into Christian churches and new elements entered the architecture. It was in this period that basilicas with double colonnades appeared and domes, representing heaven.

Constantinople was besieged by the Persians then the Arabs in the seventh century but the Empire survived except for the loss of Egypt. From the ninth to the twelfth centuries a period of cultural advancement was reflected in church architecture. Small stone built churches appeared in the shape of a cross with four arms of equal length and with a central dome. Internally, Christ was positioned centrally in the dome with the Virgin in the Apse and angels, apostles and saints placed hierarchically. The monastery at Osios Loukas was built in this period. Towards the very end of the Byzantine period churches were constructed combining the basilica and the cross structure and incorporating several small domes.

In 1204 *Constantinople* was sacked by the Fourth Crusade when the Germans, Franks and Venetians turned their armies against it. Two centuries of conflict and shifting power followed with the increasingly expansionist Turks taking over much of mainland Greece. On 29 May 1453 *Constantinople* fell to the Muslim Turks and the Turkish occupancy of Greece was all but complete, many of the islands still free fell later.

THE TURKISH RULE (1453-1830)

Memories of the Ottoman occupation, which lasted almost 400 years, still fester in the mind of the modern Greek. Greece as a nation sank into obscurity and took refuge in rural provincialism. The Greek Orthodox church was tolerated by the Islamic doctrine and designated by the Turks as a secular administrative body. By default, the church became the custodian of Greek identity. The preservation of Byzantine culture rested with the monasteries which sometimes secretly schooled the children.

Gradually the Ottoman administration started to disintegrate becoming more decentralised. In these changing circumstances some regions were achieving more autonomy, Greek merchant fleets started to grow and trade throughout the Mediterranean. Widespread resentment of Turkish rule largely remained isolated but increasing support and co-operation between rival groups finally led to the War of Independence in 1821-1822.

On 25 March 1821 the Greek flag of independence was raised at the monastery of Agia Lavra in the northern Peloponnese which is now remembered as National Independence Day. The struggle continued for some time with European public opinion enraged by the well publicised slaughter by the Turks of 25,000 Greeks on Chios and Psara. In 1827 Ioannis Kapodistrias was appointed by Greek leaders as the first president of independent Greece. His autocratic style of government was widely resented and he was assassinated in 1831. Otto, a young Bavarian prince gained support and approval to become the first King of Greece in 1833. Greek independence was confirmed by the western powers in 1830 and the borders were drawn to include part of central Greece, the Peloponnese, the Cyclades and the Argo-Saronic islands.

1

ATHENS AND ATTICA

The lure of Athens (Athena) lies in a romantic vision of an age long since past. A pastoral vision of graceful architecture, greenery and tumbling streams. The present day reality is a high density sprawl. A huge concrete monster with an insatiable appetite intent on devouring all in its path. Even the restraining hills seem in danger of being swamped. Add to this noise, dirt and pollution and one may wonder why anyone still bothers to go at all but go they do. In the middle of this concrete jungle still lie the remains of Athens' ancient glory where it is still possible to escape into the past. Byron's view of Athens in 1809 was succinctly expressed in this apt couplet and there has been no improvement since. 'Shrine of the mighty! Can it be That this is all remains of thee?'

The removal of the capital of newly liberated Greece from Nafplio to Athens in 1834 provided an ideal opportunity for improvement. There followed a period of planned building construction in neo-Classical style but dreams of repeating Pericles achievement were abruptly ended in 1922 as a result of the Greek-Turkish war in Asia Minor. The ethnic population exchange which ensued witnessed an influx of political refugees. Unable to keep pace with housing de-mands, shanty towns mushroomed in outlying areas. The problem was further aggravated by World War II followed by Civil War and a subsequent massive population movement from rural areas into the city.

Athens lies in the Attica basin surrounded by the mountains of Parnes (1,413m/4,635ft), Pendeli (1,107m/3,631ft), Hymettus (1,026m/3365ft) and Egaleo (468m/1,535ft). Its current problems are compounded by its geographical position and a population which has almost quadrupled to around four million people in the past 40 years; over a third of the population of Greece. The attendant pollution from industry and cars is trapped by the surrounding ring

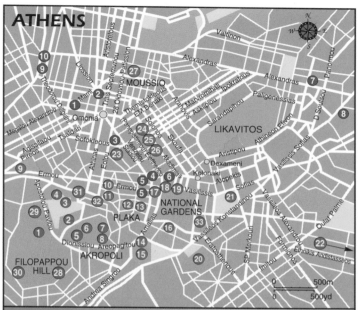

ATHENS

KEY TO STREET PLAN

Places to Visit

1 The Pynx
2 The Areopagus (Hill of Ares)
3 The Agora
4 The Temple of Hephaistos
5 The Herod Atticus Odeon
6 The Acropolis
7 Acropolis Museum
8 The Theatre of Dionysos
9 Kermeikos & Museum
10 Kapnikarea
11 Agios Eleftherios Church & Athens
Cathedral (Metropolis)
12 Popular Art & Tradition Centre
13 Popular Art Museum
14 Hadrian's Arch
15 The Temple of the Olympian Zeus
16 The Zappeion Exhibition & Congress Hall
17 Syntagma Square
18 Tomb of the Unknown Soldier
19 Greek National Parliament Building
20 The Stadium
21 War Museum
22 Monastery of Kaisariani

23 Agia Theodoria Church
24 Library
25 University
26 Academy
27 National Archaeological Museum
28 Filopappou Monument
29 Observatory
30 Filopappou Theatre
31 Flea Market (Monastiraki)
32 Tower of the Winds & Roman Agora
33 Presidential Residence (Last Royal Palace)

Public Services

1 Athens Traffic Police
2 First Aid Station
3 Antiques & Restoration Bureau
4 Greek National Tourist Office (EOT)
5 GNTO Information Desk (EOT)
6 Press & Information Bureau
7 Aliens Bureau
8 Automobile & Touring Club
9 Railway Station–Peloponnese
10 Railway Station–Northern Greece

of mountains and, in summer, the *nefos* lies like a yellow blanket over the city.

A word of warning; do not be tempted to underestimate the pollution. It is usually at its very worst during the heat of summer when traffic can sometimes be stopped for days at a time to give it chance to clear. Even the healthy can become ill so if you suffer from any respiratory complaint do not contemplate a visit then. November to April are the best months to visit with early spring perhaps the best time of all.

The major sites are confined to a relatively small area within the city centre and, with an early start, easily viewed in one day. A stay of a few days however, allows for wider exploration and a chance to discover some easily accessible oases like the delightful monastery at Kaisariani, the National Gardens and Filopappou Hill.

Driving in Athens is a nightmare of congestion, one-way systems, vague signposting, parking restrictions, wheel clamping and confiscated number plates to name but a few of the problems. For these reasons all tours in the city described, with one exception, are either by foot, on public transport or an organised trip. If you do arrive with your own car some hotels provide parking, check beforehand if possible. There are also a number of storage garages in Athens and Piraeus (details follow).

Most of the accommodation in Athens is centrally situated. Hotels close to Syntagma and Plaka providing the most convenient base for getting around on foot. There is no premium on the price of hotels in Athens compared with other parts of Greece thanks to tourist office control. For those not wishing to stay in the city there are plenty of hotels by the coast out at Glyfada, Voula and Vouliagmeni close to the airport. These coastal resorts are connected to the city by a regular bus service, a journey of about 45 minutes, but when it is very busy this can be a long hot journey.

ㄾ Tour 1 • Ancient Athens

A visit to Athens is synonymous with a visit to the **Acropolis**. As long ago as 7,000BC Stone Age man was attracted to the hill and built one of the earliest settlements in Greece on its slopes. During the Mycenaean era it was peopled by successive priest-kings and their retainers who lived in a palace on the site. The remains of cyclopean walls stem from this time. From 1100BC there followed a period of transformation which saw the decline of the palace culture of the Minoan-Mycenaean world. This Dark Age, about which little is known, lasted for several hundred years and ended with the emergence of the *polis* or Greek city-state and the beginnings of democracy. Temples to the gods of the *polis* replaced the palace and other secular buildings on the Acropolis but these were destroyed by the Persians in 480BC. Athens' brief period of glory or 'Golden Age' lasted for 32 years from 461BC during the time Pericles was head of state. Using the Delian League funds, which had been transferred by the Athenians from Delos to the Acropolis, Pericles embarked on an ambitious building plan. His construction programme was executed in an amazingly short span of time, the Parthenon itself taking only 10 years to complete. After Pericles' death Athens never regained the prosperity and growth it had enjoyed under his rule falling prey to various uses and misuses of successive conquerors.

The most pleasant way to approach the Acropolis is through Plaka, from Syntagma via Nikis, Nikodimou, Flessa and up left off Lissiou, thus avoiding the busy road which runs beneath its southern flank. A paved path, just below the Acropolis, passes an entrance to the Agora and the Areopagus, visited later in the tour, before joining the main route up to the Acropolis. Facilities close to the main entrance include a bank, post office, refreshments, cloakroom/left luggage (in season) and toilets. To avoid the sizzling heat in summer make an early start. Beware of the treacherous highly polished marble underfoot!

The Sacred Way: This ancient route (20km/12 miles) ran between the Sanctuary of Eleusis (Elefsina) passing through the ceremonial Sacred Gate, adjacent to the Dipylon Gate, and through the Agora before rising up to the Propylaia.

The Beule Gate: A Roman addition built in the third century AD and the entrance to the Acropolis site.

The Propylaia: Is the name given to the group of buildings which make up the original entrance complex. The Propylon being the actual entrance built, in this case, to resemble a temple.

The Temple of Athena Nike: An exquisite temple situated high up to the right of the Propylaia.

The Erechtheion: The Temple to Athena and Poseidon built on the most sacred part of the Acropolis. On this site the two gods were believed to have held their contest to decide who ruled Athens. Its appeal today is sight of the six graceful Karyatides (copies) and the deceptive ease with which they support the porch. The original Karyatides have been removed, one by Lord Elgin and the remainder into a protective atmosphere within the Acropolis Museum.

The Acropolis Museum: Unobtrusively built on lower ground to the east of the Parthenon. Here, in addition to various pottery finds and statues, are the original Karyatides, fragments of friezes, the Almond-Eyed Kore, the Kritios Boy, the Calf-Bearer and a sculpture of the graceful, winged figure of Athena Nike untying her sandal.

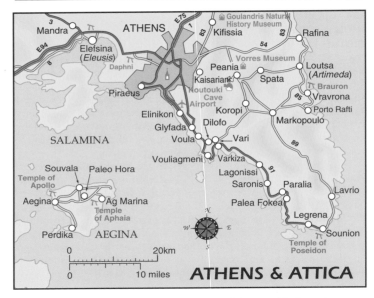

The Karyatides support the porch of the Erechtheion with deceptive ease

A splendid view of the Agora from the Acropolis

The Parthenon on the Acropolis is threatened with erosion

The Parthenon: The Temple of Athena Parthenos (Temple of the Virgin Athena) stands proudly aloof from crass modernity, despite its tumultuous history, and continues to epitomise all that was ancient Greece. Rampant erosion is the present enemy and constantly threatens to overwhelm restoration work.

The Theatre of Dionysos: The most famous theatre of the Greek world nestling into the south-east side of the hill beneath the Acropolis. Most of the present day remains are Roman.

The Asklepion: A healing sanctuary built close to the Theatre of Dionysos. A natural location considering the close relationship between drama and healing.

The Stoa of Eumenes: Constructed in the second century BC as a shelter and promenade along a section of the peripatos close to the Theatre of Dionysos. It was later connected to the Odeon of Herod Atticus by the Romans.

Odeon of Herod Atticus: Built into the south-west slope of the hill in the second century AD and restored for present day use. The Odeon is normally closed, except for performances, and the best view of it can be had from the Acropolis.

The Peripatos: The ancient road around the lower Acropolis.

The Areopagus (Hill of Ares): A small hill across a saddle to the north-west of the Acropolis hill. It was on this site the Council of Areopagus met to rule on matters of justice and in AD 51 St Paul preached the new gospel. Provides an excellent vantage point for a bird's eye view of the Agora.

The Agora: Once the hub of ancient Athenian life, now a welcome retreat. Amongst the ancient foundations stand the tenth century AD Church of the Holy Apostles and the Stoa of Attalos now rebuilt and housing a museum. On a rise in the north-west corner of the Agora is the excellently preserved Thesion or Temple of Hephaistos. From the temple there is a good view over the Agora to the Acropolis.

Tour 2 • Hill Of The Muses: Filopappou Hill and The Pnyx

Filopappou Hill, with its huge monument, and Pnyx Hill are usually only accorded a passing glance by most people as they pause in their scramble around the Acropolis. Their wooded slopes though, crisscrossed with footpaths, provide a welcome retreat from the city heat. The reward for a walk up to the monument is a clear view of the Acropolis and over the city.

Follow the same route through Plaka as for Tour 1 but continue on the main path down to Dionissiou Areopagitou road. Cross the road and head right towards the roundabout from where a cobbled road leads up onto Filopappou Hill and over to the Filopappou Theatre.

Filopappou Hill: Known also as the 'Hill of the Muses' provides extensive walkways amongst its tree clad slopes. Follow a path off left of the cobbled road to take you up to the huge monument dedicated to a Roman senator and consul, Filopappos. On the way up there are pleasant areas with old marble seats where you can rest and drink in the views over Athens. Heading back down towards the Pnyx, pass the Prison of Socrates and the Byzantine church of Ag Demetrios with its original frescos.

Pnyx Hill: Questions relating to public policy were debated by the Athenian Assembly on this hill. The area is now used for a Sound and Light show in summer. On the south-west side of the hill is a large picnic area with tables and drinking water fountains. Extensive views stretch beyond Piraeus to the sea.

Hill of the Nymphs: The site of the Observatory and gardens. Only occasionally open to the public.

Tour 3 • City Panorama

The narrow streets off sophisticated Kolonaki Square teem with boutiques for the fashion conscious and, without the constant roar of traffic, drinking coffee and people watching could be a pleasant pastime at one of the pavement cafés in the square itself. On the plus side, a rarely encountered feature are public toilets kept in pristine condition. The 15 minutes walk to Likavitos funicular station starts from this square and takes you up through Dexameni Square with its quieter ambience. **Likavitos Hill** (277m/909ft), the ultimate destination, is the highest point in Athens and the place to go for a complete panoramic view over the city and beyond. It is particularly renowned for viewing spectacular sunsets. Start your wander up pedestrianised Skoufa and on the corner of Iraklitou, where you turn right, is 'Everest' one of the best take-away food shops in the area.

Head up into leafy Dexameni Square with its outdoor café tables and the site of a reservoir begun by the Emperor Hadrian. Continue along Dinokratous as far as Ploutarchou. A left turn here will take you directly up to the funicular station for the 2 minutes ascent of Likavitos. One of the many footpaths and the most direct (15 minutes) starts 2 minutes along to the west of the station. The winding path passes a café/bar around halfway up and emerges by the small white chapel dedicated to St George, on the very top above a restaurant. An alternative path down from the lower terrace leads past the Likavitos Theatre used for Greek Dance performances in summer.

Fresh coconut, one of the more unusual snacks sold by street vendors

The salepi *seller.* Salepi *is a milk made from the tubers of wild orchids and is believed to be an aphrodisiac*

Colourful balloons for sale in Athens

A street entertainer in Plaka, Athens

🏛 Tour 4 • Museums

One thing Athens is not short of is museums. There are more than enough to keep the most ardent buff going throughout a long holiday. This programme highlights just two. The not to be missed National Museum and the fascinating Goulandris Natural History Museum out at Kifissia. Those with an appetite for more might like to consider the closely grouped Benaki Museum for Greek folk art and handicrafts, Museum of Cycladic and Ancient Greek Art, Byzantine Museum and War Museum on Vasilissis Sofias Avenue. The National Gallery is located in front of the Hilton Hotel and there are many small galleries to be found in the city centre.

The National Archaeological Museum: Situated north of Omonia Square in Patission, this vast museum demands at least a good half-day of your time. Time, and lots of it, is required to fully appreciate the sheer quality of artistry in such volume. To reap the benefit of a visit you do need a guide or a detailed guide book as the wonderful exhibits are unimaginatively displayed and labelling is almost non existent. Despite these drawbacks, the displays are housed in defined areas of the museum. By far the biggest draw is the Mycenaean Hall (Room 4) housing Schliemann's gold finds from Mycenae including what he wrongly believed to be the gold death mask of Agamemnon. How long they will remain on display in Athens is a moot point as they are scheduled to be rehoused in an on-site museum at Mycenae. Amongst the Classical Art collection can be found the bronze fifth-century BC Statue of Poseidon (Room 15) and the Little Jockey (Room 21) both reclaimed from the sea off Evia. Lifelike sculptures of the Youth of Antikythera (Room 28) and the heads of a Boxer, Philosopher and Man from Delos with his superbly captured poignant expression (Room 30). A naked Aphrodite (Room 31) excites a great deal of attention but the many sensitively sculpted Stelai provide an insight into the everyday life of the people of the time. Also not to be missed are the fantastic Thira frescos, upstairs in Room 48, restored to their original position on the walls to show how they would have looked about 3,450 years ago. Add to this rooms full of pottery and smaller finds plus an extensive Numismatic Collection, in a separate museum, on the first floor and you will almost certainly be left with the feeling that you have not been able to give full justice to your visit. The Numismatic Museum can be entered from outside, from Tositsa, or from inside the Archaeological Museum on payment of a separate entrance fee.

The Goulandris Natural History Museum: A 35-minute journey north on the metro takes you as far as its last stop, the pleasant, leafy suburb of Kifissia where this delightful and excellent museum is situated. Interesting and informative displays make it a pleasant and worthwhile trip out from the city centre for adults and children alike. To locate the museum, about a 10-minute walk, turn left outside the station along Dragoumi. Reach a T-junction and turn right into Othonos. Keep ahead across the busy mainroad at traffic lights and continue to the next T- junction where you turn right into Levithou. The museum is sited in the large house immediately on the right.

The museum is divided up into easily viewed sections starting with plants. A big three-dimensional model of a plant cell sets the tone for this simplified but highly accurate display, set up in collaboration with the Natural History Department of the British Museum in London. Insects comprises a collection of thousands of insects from all parts of mainland Greece and the islands. Birds are displayed in lifelike settings and there is even a cast of the fossilised remains of Archaeopteryx said to be the first bird that appeared on earth. The three main groups of mammals are explained and there is a fascinating collection of amphibians and reptiles. Here is an opportunity to learn how to identify the different species of tortoise to be found in the Greek countryside. Last but not least are sections covering dinosaurs, molluscs and other invertebrates, fossils and minerals and rocks. There is a café and shop in the museum.

Tour 5 • Old Athens

A stroll round Plaka's narrow streets conjures up a romantic image of an age past and is particularly atmospheric in the evening. Monastiraki on the other hand is a noisier more bustling quarter during the day and the location of the Flea Market but for a little solitude escape to the site of Athens' ancient cemetery, Kerameikos.

Start out from Syntagma Square (Platia Syntagmatos) down Mitropoleos, which leads past the Cathedral to Monastiraki, and turn left up Nikis to locate the souvenir shopping streets of Kidathineon and Adrianou.

Plaka, the oldest residential area in Athens on the lower northern slope of the Acropolis Hill, is a pleasure to explore. Its many narrow streets and alleyways hiding a few quiet backwaters especially in Anafiotika where mid-nineteenth-century construction workers from the island of Anafi built their homes. Busy, pedestrianised Kidathineon and Adrianou are lined with numerous souvenir shops their wares spilling out onto the streets in a kaleidoscope of colour. Adrianou stretches from the Thesion by the Ancient Agora almost to Hadrian's Arch passing the metro station at Monastiraki and the Monument of Lysicrates which carried the bronze tripod he won in a drama contest. Squeezed into an area off Adrianou at its junction with Eolou, below the Acropolis, is the Roman Agora and the first century BC Tower of the Winds, a water clock, compass, weather vane and sundial. As a change from shopping there are the Popular Arts Museum, Popular Arts and Traditions Centre and an open-air cinema. Tavernas and cafés abound for mellow evenings spent eating and drinking in one of Plaka's leafy squares to the sound of a bouzouki or, for more robust Greek evenings, in a night club environment.

Merging into Plaka, **Monastiraki** and its bazaar-like atmosphere is where to head for a taste of more authentic Greek life, especially to the west of Monastiraki square. The **Flea Market** starts down Pandrossou which runs from the bottom corner of the cathedral square on Mitropoleos. Along this more touristy section can be found the 'poet-sandalmaker' of Athens, Stavros Melissinos, who made sandals for John Lennon of 'The Beatles' fame. Across Monastiraki Square the Flea Market fills narrow Ifestou with an amazing array of goods for sale and exudes a more homespun air. The square itself has been the core of a market area since Turkish times. A past which is still very much alive today in the cacophony of sound from barrel-organ players to the many street vendors touting lottery tickets, nuts, fruit, drinks and various snack foods. Every Sunday the Flea Market cascades into the surrounding streets attracting throngs of Athenians in search of a bargain. Even the Flower Market, close to the Church of Ag Irini (St Irene) a little way up Eolou, becomes drawn into the carnival-like atmosphere.

Entered from Ermou and tucked into the wedge of land between Ermou and Pireos lies **Kerameikos** a little visited and unexpectedly peaceful haven. This is the site of the main cemetery of ancient Athens where the ruins of the Long Walls, which ran to the port at Piraeus, and the Dipylon and Sacred Gates can be seen. Some plots have been excavated and their original or replica stones replaced in position. Terracotta figurines, vases and intricately sculpted stelai form an extensive collection of finds from the site which are housed in the on-site Oberlaender Museum.

Tour 6 • Shopping And Byzantine Churches

Compared with most other major cities Athens' shopping centre is contained within a relatively small area. Situated on the north side and adjacent to the city's ancient quarter, it is easily accessible to most tourist hotels. Also to be found in the same area are a clutch of Byzantine churches all fighting for survival amidst the concrete and car exhaust fumes. The suggested route provides a good overview but, with more time to spare, further exploration of narrow streets like Leka and Praxitelous are worthwhile.

Syntagma Square makes a good starting point for a shopping expedition and is also where airline and tour company offices can be located. Ferries and organised trips can be booked at travel agents along Filelinon and Nikis on the Plaka side of Mitropoleos en route to Athens Cathedral (Metropolis) which dwarfs its much more interesting predecessor the twelfth-century AD church of Ag Eleftherios.

Leave the Cathedral Square along Evangelistrias to reach the clothing shops and Byzantine **Church of Kapnikarea**, now a traffic island in the middle of the road, on Ermou. Escape the traffic by turning up towards Omonia into a pedestrianised section of Eolou to pass the colourful Flower Market alongside the **Church of Ag Irini**. Spare time also to pause and look back for the best view of the Tower of the Winds against the backdrop of the Acropolis hill before turning left towards Athinas on reaching Evripidou. (Diverting briefly right at this point leads to the **Church of Ag Theodori** at the end of Evripidou.) A right turn into Athinas and the clamour of human activity competes with the roar of traffic around the Meat and Fish Market on the right and the Fruit and Vegetable Market on the left. Past the markets on the right is fenced off **Kotzia Square**, containing excavated remains, around which a Greek version of a car boot sale is held on Sundays.

Hurtling traffic, squealing tyres and scurrying crowds epitomise **Omonia Square**, the heart of the student quarter. Traffic converges from many directions, circling the controversial glass statue of an olympic runner on the island in the centre, most of it heading down Ag Konstantinou in the direction of Corinth and the Peloponnese or Pireos to Piraeus. Passageways and arcades lined with shops and quick-food outlets run off the square and provide a welcome diversion from the constant noise and congestion. The larger department stores are also situated in the vicinity.

The route continues out to the east of Omonia Square crossing Ermou then back down Eleftheriou Venizelou, better known as Panepistimiou, in the direction of Syntagma. Three buildings of note stand side by side about half way down on the left the **Library** (Bibliothiki), the **University** (Panepistimiou) and the **Academy** (Akadimia). They are easy to pass by and admire from a distance but frescos depicting the arts and science which adorn the porch of the University are worth a pause. The photogenic and pristine façade of the Academy gives the appearance of having been plucked straight out of an ancient Greek setting.

❋ The fashionable shopping area around **Kolonaki Square** almost completes the circuit. As a change from designer boutiques, a lively fruit, flower and vegetable street market is held close by on Friday mornings along Xenokratous.

Tour 7 • Constitutional Heart

Syntagma or Constitution Square with its garden and cafés is possibly the most familiar square and meeting point in Athens. The ❋ sentries guarding the **Tomb of the Unknown Soldier** outside the Parliament building draw the crowds but fewer people venture into the restful ambience of the National Gardens close by. Built between ❋ 1834 and1838 as a palace for Greece's King Otho, the **Greek National Parliament Building** or 'Vouli' looks disdainfully down over Syntagma Square. The focus of interest though is not the building but the ceremonial guards or *evzones* who stand guard at the front. With their unusual costumes, based on those of the *klefts* from northern Greece, and their strange clockwork movements they are a constant source of fascination. Every Sunday at 11am there is an official changing of the guard when a troop of soldiers, all dressed in their 'best' uniforms, march on parade accompanied by a band.

❋ The **National Gardens** (Ethnikos Kipos) spread out behind the Parliament building. Access from Syntagma is along Leoforos Amalias or up Vassilissis Sofias past the flower sellers. First designed, landscaped and planted between 1839 and 1860 they became the first Royal Gardens of King Otho and Queen Amalia. Dedicated more to ornamental plants than flowers, there are more than 500 species and varieties most of which are not native. During a period of democracy in 1927 the gardens were renamed the National Gardens and opened to the public. Signposted footpaths weave through tangled foliage which creates a cooling protective canopy from the relentless summer sun. Tucked away amidst this greenery is a Botanical Museum, close to the Parliament building, tranquil pools and what could be loosely termed a menagerie.

The rear of a large crescent shaped building, the Zappeion, and a wide boulevard mark the southern end of the gardens. The **Zappeion** was built especially for the 1896 Olympic Games by the Zappas family. It was used to house the competitors and effectively became the first Olympic village of modern times. At the front side of the building, closest to Irodou Attikou (Herod Atticus Street), is the famous 'Aigli' café/restaurant/ open-air cinema complex but only the café is open year round.

To the east of the Zappeion at the junction of Irodou Attikou and

Vassileos Konstandinou is the **Stadium** (Stadiou). It was rebuilt over ✻
its ancient predecessor for the 1896 Olympic Games but is too narrow
for competitive use today. A short way up Irodou Attikou is the last
Royal and now the Presidential Palace where more *evzones* can be
seen on guard outside.

South from the Zappeion leads through the Zappeion Gardens
and crosses Leoforos Olgas to the **Temple of Olympian Zeus** and 𝝠
Hadrian's Arch. The temple, completed by Hadrian, was the largest
Corinthian temple in Greece with 104 columns of which only four-
teen remain standing today. **Hadrian's Arch** was erected by him to 𝝠
mark the boundary between 'the city of Theseus' and 'the city of
Hadrian'. Something of their former glory is restored at night when
they can be viewed floodlit.

Tour 8 • The Monastery Of Kaisariani

Peace and solitude lie no more than 5½km (3 miles) from the heart of
Athens at Kaisariani (Kessariani). The grounds of this eleventh-
century monastery, on the lower slopes of Mount Hymettus, are a
botanists' delight and an ideal setting for a picnic even when the
monastery itself is closed. Raised above the infamous 'nefos' by its
position at a height of 450m (1,476ft) above sea level it is arguably the
loveliest country site closest to the city. If quietness is a priority avoid
weekends and holidays.

Take blue bus number 224 to Kaisariani, boarding at the first blue
shelter up Vassilissis Sofias, to the left of the Parliament building.
The monastery is a 2½km (1½ miles) walk of about 30 to 40 minutes
from the terminus so it is advisable to take refreshments as there are
no shops or cafés en route or at the monastery. Stay on the bus for the
15 to 20 minutes bus journey as far as the terminus. Walk back to the
road the bus has just left, turn right, and continue up the road with
the cemetery on your right. There is no pavement but once past the
cemetery a path winds through the trees alongside the road to the
right. Flower lovers will definitely want to linger in spring to inspect
the scattering of flowers along the way including the bee orchids
Ophrys lutea, O. fusca and the beautiful saw-fly orchid *O.
tenthredinifera*. Amongst the Orchis species are the delicate *Orchis
quadripunctata* and the fascinating naked-man orchid *O. italica*.
Standing above all is the giant orchid, *Barlia robertiana*, which can
reach a height of half a metre. Muscari species also abound but
difficult to spot amongst the foliage is *Fritillaria graeca* and the iris-
like *Hermodactylus tuberosus*.

Keep right to pass under the motorway bridge. The road continues

A ceremonial changing of the guard takes place every Sunday outside the Greek National Parliament Building, Athens

The pristine façade of the Hellenic Academy, Athens

directly to the monastery but by far the more interesting route is to turn immediately right now up the steps alongside the motorway. Take the path up diagonally left, just before the paved area ends by the motorway, which runs into a stronger path. Keep left, rising steadily, with the motorway now behind. More of the same flowers brighten the way but keep up right at a fork in the path and climb a little more steeply before crossing a track. Soon after, before the next bend, take the well defined path up to the left. Rise up into a clearing where there are the ruins of the tenth- century AD Church of the Assomaton Taxiarchon and chapel of St Mark. To the right is a pine fringed picnic area from where there is a wonderful panorama over Athens.

Continue on the path past the ruins and descend on the far side towards the monastery which can now be seen through the trees ahead. Conservationists will be pleased to learn that Athens Friends of the Trees Society are responsible for the upkeep of the cypress, pine, plane, olive, almond, apple and eucalyptus trees which shade the site. Stepping into the leafy enclosure which houses the monastery and its two churches is a refreshing world away from the twentieth century turmoil outside. On the opposite side of the monastery to the entrance is a ram's head fountain. It is fed by waters from a spring, a little higher up, which was once purported to enhance fertility. The same spring also used to supply Athens with drinking water.

Return to the bus terminus via the same route or down the road. On the ride back into Athens the Hilton Hotel provides a timely reminder that the bus is entering Vassilissis Sofia. Alight opposite the War Museum, as the bus then shoots off to the right into a maze of back streets away from Syntagma.

Tour 9 • Daphni And Eleusis (Elefsina)

Follow the route of the Sacred Way to the site of the Sanctuary of Demeter and its famed Eleusinian Mysteries. Stop off at Daphni, the half way point, to admire the mosaics in one of the oldest Byzantine monasteries.

Blue buses (ticket only) for Daphni and Elefsina depart from Platia Eleftherias, off Pireos, at frequent intervals. Numbers 853, 854, 855, 862 and 880 start from close to the corner where Dipilou and Milerou cross.

The bus roughly follows the route of the Sacred Way through uninspiring suburbs and industrialisation. A more country atmosphere and the sight of castellated walls, after a journey of about 20 minutes, heralds your arrival at Daphni.

Approach the monastery down the wide track across the road from the bus stop. **Daphni** was named after the laurels, sacred to Apollo, which grew in the area. His Sanctuary stood on the same site and remnants from that building were incorporated into the construction of the boundary wall and the monastery. Rebuilt in the eleventh century AD little remains of the earlier fifth-century AD structure dedicated to the Virgin Mary. Fragmentary remains of mosaics and newly restored frescos are worth viewing. A Wine Festival is held in the grounds each year.

Continue by bus a further 20 minutes along the Sacred Way to **Eleusis** at **Elefsina**. Ask for Arkaos (Ancient) Eleusis. To locate the site look for a fluttering Greek flag atop an elevated pale blue clock tower. Walk along the street and through a pedestrianised platia to the site entrance which is on the left. The surroundings might be industrial but the attractive site, on the slopes of a low rocky hill, manages to distance itself from present day intrusion. In the museum is a model of the layout of the Sanctuary of Demeter which helps give substance to the many foundations.

The Sanctuary at Eleusis was a centre for the worship of Demeter — Kore, the Earth Mother and her daughter Persephone. Greeks believed the Eleusinian Mysteries held the universe together and that life would end without them so they were also connected with cycles of lunar and solar movements. Initiates, sworn to a vow of secrecy, underwent rituals which centred around death and rebirth, in their quest for immortality. Return to Athens from the bus stop on the main road.

Tour 10 • Koutouki Cave And Vorres Museum

Mount Hymettus hides a different face on its eastern slope from the one most usually viewed from Athens. Stark it may be, when compared with its softer lower slopes to the west, but visitors to the cave are rewarded with sweeping views across the Mesogeia Plain eastwards over the coast to Evia and beyond.

Catch a blue bus number 125 or 310 for the 50 minute journey to **Peania**, (Paiania) from the terminus at Thissio close by the junction of Eptahalkou and Apostolou Pavlou. Ask to be told when you reach the platia in Peania where you can catch a taxi for the 5km (3miles) up to **Koutouki Cave**.

There are conducted tours of the cave every half-hour which take about 20 minutes. It is advisable to wear suitable footwear as the floor is fairly wet and can be slippery. Inside the cave the concealed lighting highlights the more spectacular stalactite and stalagmite formations enhancing the varied hues and shades of colour in the rock formations. The green coloration is man induced; it is algae growth in response to the artificial illumination. A sound and light finale where the changing colour temperature of light is sequenced to match that of natural daylight, a rosy dawn for example, makes a fitting end to the visit. Refreshments and souvenirs are available and there is a large terrace on which to sit and admire the views.

Return to Peania and, if it is weekend, there is the opportunity to visit the **Vorres Museum** and gardens. The museum, situated near the square, houses what began as a private collection of Greek art and covers a variety of styles as far back as Mycenaean times.

Tour 11 • The Apollo Coast

Pink hued dawns and blazing golden-red sunsets create a mystical aura around the majestic white marble Temple of Poseidon at Cape Sounion. A commanding landmark down the centuries for sailors approaching the Saronic Gulf from the Aegean and, more recently, for air travellers on the descent into Athens airport.

It is a 65km (40 mile) winding run down the Apollo Coast to Cape Sounion. Orange buses leave Athens regularly from Mavromateon at its junction with Leoforos Alexandras (south-west corner of Areos Park) for the trip down to Sounion. The quicker bus goes via the coast road and the other via Markopoulo and Lavrio through the middle of Attica. Either can be a long hot journey especially in summer. The advantages of hiring a car are that you can stop where you like when you like. The disadvantages are more noticeable in summer when the coast road is crowded and driving slow. The most comfortable way to go is on an organised trip on an air-conditioned coach run by companies such as CHAT, KEY and GO and with an accompanying guide who dispenses interesting information en route as well as leading a guided tour of the site.

Exit Athens along Leoforos Syngrou for the $1\frac{1}{2}$ hour drive to Sounion. Go left at Old Faliron on approaching the coast. The island of Aegina is clearly visible in the gulf to the right as the coast is followed down in the direction of the west airport at Elinikon. Once past the airport the area becomes visibly more upmarket. Glyfada, with its fish restaurants and high class shops and apartments where wealthy Athenians spend their weekends, merges with Voula. After Voula where the road divides keep to the longer and prettier coastal road. The inland road, to the left through Dilofo and Vari, is lined with tavernas frequented by Greeks who flock there for specialities such as suckling pig and goat. Continue following the coast through

Tranquility at Kaisariani, close to Athens centre

The Temple of Poseidon at Sounion

Vouliagmeni passing the Astir Beach promontory which is the site of the sixth-century BC Temple of Apollo from which the Apollo Coast gets its name.

Exclusive beach homes are more in evidence now as the dense building development closer to Athens is left behind. After Varkiza, where the shorter road through Vari rejoins, the route continues close to the coast through the smaller resorts of Lagonissi, Saronis and Palea Fokea which are popular with the Athenians. Buildings give way to rolling phrygana covered hills and the white columns of the Temple of Poseidon soon come into view ahead.

The **Temple of Poseidon** sits 60m (197ft) above the sea on the highest point of **Cape Sounion**. A fitting setting for the god of the wild sea and earthquakes. An earlier temple from the sixth-century BC stood on the site until it was destroyed by the Persians. The present temple was constructed at the same time as the Parthenon in the same Doric style but smaller. Today only sixteen of its thirty four columns remain standing. It is possible to make out the foundations of a small temple dedicated to Athena Sounias, the protector of Attika, on the isthmus connecting the cape to the mainland.

To really capture the mood of the site you need to visit early in the morning or in the evening. In spring there is the added delight of wild flowers amongst the mass of yellow *Medicago arborea* bushes. There is a feeling of being surrounded by the sea from the terrace of the café adjoining the site but be prepared to pay over the odds for a beer. **Lavrio**, which used to be an important centre for silver mining, is 10km (6 miles) further along the coast from Sounion. Ferries from Lavrio to the Island of Kea, more popularly known as Tzia, leave daily.

Tour 12 • The Island Of Aegina

An opportunity to enjoy refreshing sea breezes and swim in clear turquoise green water; to sample octopus, pistachios and the local retsina and visit the beautiful wooded site of the Temple of Aphaia from where there are fine views out over the Saronic Gulf. Aegina is one of the most ancient kingdoms of Greece and the first, albeit temporary, capital of Greece in 1828 before the seat of government was transferred to Nafplio then later Athens.

Ferry boats and hydrofoils ply daily between the main harbour at Piraeus and Aegina Town. The former takes 1½ hours and the latter 35 minutes. In summer there is a ferry service directly to **Ag Marina** which is convenient for visitors to the Temple of Aphaia. Tickets for ferry and hydrofoil are available from different kiosks close to where they depart. Take the metro to the harbour at Piraeus (Pireas) which takes about 15 to 20 minutes. Leave the station by the bottom exit and turn left for the 5 to 10 minutes walk to the harbour. Cross the road towards the seafront and the left-hand side of the bus station in Platia Karaiskaki. On reaching the harbour, look for the ferry and hydrofoil to the left.

On arrival in **Aegina Town** book your return ticket, especially in high season for the hydrofoil, from the kiosk on the harbour. The narrow streets are lively and colourful with souvenir shops, tavernas and a small fish market. On a headland to the left as you reach the harbour is the site of the Temple of Apollo which is open to the public. Just beyond the temple site is a narrow sand and shingle beach backed by pine and tamarisk trees which shade a pleasant picnic area.

Buses and taxis are located to the left as you disembark on arrival. It is advisable to arrive on the island early in the day as buses are more frequent in the morning. The bus to the main resort town of Ag Marina (25 minutes), with its sandy beach, passes close to the island's ruined old capital Paleohora before reaching the **Temple of Aphaia**. This late sixth century BC Doric construction, which was built on the site of two earlier temples, stands on a hill amidst pine trees about 3km (2 miles) outside Ag Marina. Many parts of the temple have been preserved or restored and with twenty four of the original thirty two columns now standing it is an impressive sight. Aphaia was an ancient goddess and patroness of Aegina but was replaced by the better known Athena at the time of the Trojan War. Thus the temple is known today as the Aphaia-Athena. The fishing village of Perdika to the south is also accessible by bus from Aegina Town (20 minutes).

Eastern Attica

The whole of the east coast of Attica is fast developing as a playground for Athenians who shun the glitz and glamour of Glyfada and Vouliagmeni. There is nothing much to attract the visitor to the central region except for those with an insatiable appetite for Byzantine churches. Hiring a car for two days would allow time for a visit to Sounion and the lesser sites of Amfiaraion, Ramnous, Marathon and Vravrona (Brauron).

Additional Information

Places to Visit

Athens

Acropolis Archaeological Site
Open: Monday-Friday 8am-5pm
Saturday-Sunday & Holidays
8.30am-3pm.

Acropolis Museum
Open: Monday 11am-5pm.
Tuesday-Friday 8am-5pm.
Saturday-Sunday & Holidays
8.30am-3pm.

*Ancient Agora, Thision and Stoa of
   Attalus Museum*
Open: Tuesday-Sunday & Holidays
8.30am-3pm. Closed Monday.

Benaki Museum
1 Koumbari & Vas Sofias, Open:
Monday-Sunday & Holidays
8.30am-2pm. Closed Tuesday.

Byzantine Museum
22 Vas Sofias
Open: Tuesday-Sunday & Holidays
8.30am-3pm. Closed Monday.

Centre of Folk Art and Tradition
6 Hatzimihali (off Kidathineon)
Free entry. Open Tuesday, Thu
9am-9pm Wednesday, Friday,
Saturday 9am-1pm & 5-9pm
Sunday & Holidays 9am-1pm.
Closed Monday.

Dionysus Theatre
Open: Monday 11am-5pm,
Tuesday-Friday 8am-5pm.
Saturday, Sunday & Holidays
8.30am-3pm.

Greek Folk Art Museum
17 Kidathineon
Open: Tuesday-Sunday & Holidays
10am-2pm. Closed Monday.

*Kerameikos Archaeological Site and
   Museum*
148 Ermou
Open: Monday 11am-5pm.
Tuesday-Friday 8am-5pm.
Saturday, Sunday & Holidays
8.30am-3pm.

National Archaeological Museum
44 Patission
Open: Monday 11am-5pm.
Tuesday-Friday 8am-5pm.
Saturday, Sunday & Holidays
8.30am-3pm.

Numismatic Museum
1 Tossitsa
Open: Tuesday-Sunday & Holidays
8.30am-3pm. Closed Monday.

Roman Agora
Open: Tuesday-Sunday & Holidays
8.30am-3pm. Closed Monday.

Temple of the Olympian Zeus
Vas. Olgas & Amalias
Open: Tuesday-Sunday & Holidays
8.30am-3pm. Closed Monday.

War Museum of Greece
Vas. Sofias & Rizari
Open: Tuesday-Saturday 9am-
2pm. Sunday & Holidays 9.30am-
2pm. Closed Monday.

Athens Suburbs
Daphni Monastery
Open: Monday-Sunday & Holidays
8.30am-3pm.

*Eleusis (Elefsina) Archaeological Site
   & Museum*
Open: Tuesday-Sunday & Holidays
8.30am-3pm. Closed Monday.

Kaisariani Monastery
Open: Tuesday, Sunday & Holidays
8.30am-3pm. Closed Monday.

Kifissia, Goulandris Natural History Museum
13 Levidou
Open: Monday-Sunday & Holidays
9am-2.30pm. Closed Friday.

Aegina (Island)

Temple of Aphaia
Open: Monday-Friday 8am-5pm.
Saturday, Sunday & Holidays
8.30am-3pm.

Temple of Apollo & Aegina Museum
Open: Daily 8.30am-3pm.
Closed Monday.

Attica

Kalamos, Amfiaraio Archaeological Site
Open: Monday-Sunday & Holidays
8.30am-3pm.

Marathonas Tomb Museum
Open: Tuesday-Sunday & Holidays
8.30am-3pm. Closed Monday.

Peania, Vorres Museum
Open: Saturday, Sunday &
Holidays only 10am-2pm.

Ramnous Archaeological Site
Kato Souli
Open: Tuesday-Sunday & Holidays
8.30am-3pm. Closed Monday.

Sounion (Sounio), Temple of Poseidon
Open: daily & Holidays 10am-
Sunset.

Vravrona Archaeological Site
(Brauron) Open: Tuesday-Sunday
& Holidays 9am-2.30pm. Closed
Monday.

Vravrona Museum
Open: Tuesday-Sunday & Holidays
8.30am-3pm. Closed Monday.

Useful Information

Athens
POST OFFICE
The Post Offices located at Omonia
Square, Syntagma Square and the
Acropolis are open on Sundays
from 9am-1.30pm in addition to
their normal weekday opening
hours. There is also a mobile Post
Office at Monastiraki Square open
weekdays 8am-6pm and Sundays
from 8am-5pm.

LOCAL TRANSPORT
Buses run from 5am-12midnight.

Buses
Blue: Athens & Suburbs from
various stops in centre.
Green: Athens to Piraeus. Yellow
'trolleys'. A flat rate fare applies for
the above 'ticket only' services and
tickets, singly or in tens, are
available from kiosks throughout
Athens. Validate in ticket machine
as enter vehicle.
Orange: Attica destinations. Most
start from Mavromateon Street.
Blue & Yellow double-decker: 24-
hour frequent express lines A & *A*
and B & *B* from the East and West
air terminals stopping at Syntagma
(Amalias Ave) and Omonia
(Stadiou St) to Bus Terminals A
and B and return. The B & *B* lines
pass the main railway stations. Port
of Piraeus to airports #19.

Bus Terminals (K.T.E.L.)
Well north of the city centre but
frequent bus links.
A: 100, Kifissou Street. Buses to
Western and Southern Greece and
the Ionian Islands. (Bus No. 051
every 10 minutes from the corner
of Zinonos & Menandrou near
Omonia. From 5am-12midnight).

B: 260 Liossion Street (Closest to railway stations). Buses to Northern and Eastern Greece and Evia. (Bus No. 024 every 15 minutes from Amalias, in front of the entrance to the National Gardens. From 5am-12midnight. The nearest Metro stop is Ag Nicholaos).

Railway Stations
Stathmos Peloponissou: for the Peloponnese.
Stathmos Larissis: Northern Greece. (Trolley Bus No #1 or Express Buses B & B from in front of the Parliament Building).

Metro
Piraeus to Kifissia. Runs from 5.30am-12midnight.
Validate tickets in machines at barriers. Journey times: Omonia - Piraeus 20 minutes. Omonia - Kifissia 30 minutes.
Stations: Piraeus (port) - Neo Faliro - Moschato - Kallithea - Tavros - El. Venizelos - Petralona - Thissio - Monastiraki - Omonia - Victoria - Attiki - Ag Nikolaos - Kato Patissia - Ag Eleftherios - Patissia - Perissos - Pefkakia - Nea Ionia - Iraklio - Irini - Maroussi - K.A.T. - Kifissia.

Hydrofoil (Flying Dolphins)
Tickets from office on quay at point of departure or, in season, it is advisable to book ahead in Athens. Enquire at EOT for where to book. Buy return ticket on arrival at destination. Daily service direct to Aegina from Piraeus close by Akti Tzelepi, 5-10 minutes walk from the metro. Services to Poros, Hydra and Spetses (Nafplion and Monemvasia in season) depart from the Zea Marina, 20 minutes walk from metro.

Accommodation

HOTELS
There is no shortage of hotels and pensions in Athens from luxury (L) through to E class. The following list is just a small sample of what is on offer. Accommodation listed for Athens is close to Plaka and all listed below are open all year. Hotel bookings can be made at the Hellenic Chamber of Hotels office at 2 Karegeorgis Servias Street. Syntagma, Athens (National Bank of Greece building) during opening hours. Also available from this address is a comprehensive list of hotels in Attica.

ATHENS: TELEPHONE PREFIX 01
Hotel Astir Palace (L)
Panepistimiou & Vas Sofias
106 71 Athens
☎ 3643112/9

Athens Hilton Hotel (L)
46 Vas Sofias
106 76 Athens
☎ 7220201/10

Grande Bretagne Hotel (L)
Syntagma Square
05 63 Athens
☎ 3230251/9, 3250701/9

Hotel Ledra Marriott (L)
113-115, Syngrou
117 45 Athens
☎ 9347711

Hotel Amalia (A)
10 Amalias
105 57 Athens
☎ 3237301/9

Hotel Electra Palace (A)
18 Nikodimou
105 57 Athens
☎ 3241401/7

Hotel Herodio (A)
4 Rovertou Galli
117 42 Athens
☎ 9236832/36

Olympic Palace (A)
16 Filellinon
105 57 Athens
☎ 3237611, 3237615

Hotel Ilissos (B)
72 Kallirois
117 45 Athens
☎ 9223523/9, 9223927/9

Hotel Omiros (B)
15 Apollonos
105 57 Athens
☎ 3235486/7

Hotel Aphrodite (C)
21 Apollonos
105 57 Athens
☎ 3234357/9, 3226047

Hotel Austria (C)
7 Mousiou
117 42 Athens
☎ 9235151/3, 9220777 (Reserv.)

Hotel Hermes (C)
19 Apollonos
105 57 Athens
☎ 3235514/6

Hotel Imperial (C)
46 Mitropoleos
105 63 Athens
☎ 3227617/6, 3227780

Hotel Nefeli (C)
16 Iperidou, Plaka
105 58 Athens
☎ 3228044/5

Hotel Niki (C)
27 Nikis
105 57 Athens
☎ 3220913/5, 3220886

PIRAEUS: TELEPHONE PREFIX 01
Hotel Noufara (B)
45 Iroon Politehniou
185 33 Piraeus
☎ 4115541/3

Hotel Savoy (B)
93 Iroon Politehniou
185 36 Piraeus
☎ 4131102/8

Hotel Triton (B)
8 Tsamadou
185 31 Piraeus
☎ 4173457/8

Hotel Anemoni (C)
65-67 Evripidou, 185 33 Piraeus
☎ 4111768, 4130091

Hotel Argo (C)
23 Notara
185 31 Piraeus
☎ 4121795/6, 4121918

Hotel Cavo (C)
79-81 Filonos 185 35 Piraeus
☎ 4116134/5, 4175290, 4110235

GLYFADA: TELEPHONE PREFIX 01
Congo Palace Hotel (A)
75 Possidonos
166 74 Glyfada
☎ 8946711/5

Palace Hotel (A)
4 Possidonos
166 75 Glyfada
☎ 8948361, 8946068, 8980847

Hotel Fenix (B)
1 Artemissiou
166 75 Glyfada
☎ 8981255/9

Hotel Golden Sun (B)
72 J. Metaxa
166 74 Glyfada
☎ 8981353/6, 8981974

Hotel Avra (C)
5 Lambraki
166 75 Glyfada
☎ 8947185, 8946452, 8946264, 8941111

Hotel Perla (C)
Possidono & 7 Hrissidos
166 75 Glyfada
☎ 8944212/4

VOULA: TELEPHONE PREFIX 01
Hotel Castello Beach (B)
8 Kerkiras & Aktis
166 73 Voula
☎ 8958985, 8959533

Hotel Plaza (B)
17 Alkionidon
166 73 Voula
☎ 8953575, 8990007

Hotel Minerva (C)
2 Metaxa & Vas Georgiou
166 73 Voula ☎ 8953186

**VOULIAGMENI: TELEPHONE PREFIX 01
POST CODE 166 71**
Nafsika Astir Palace Hotel (L)
☎ 8960211/9

Hotel Armonia (A)
1 Armonias
☎ 8960105, 8960030

Hotel Margi House (A)
11 Litous
☎ 8962061/5

Hotel Blue Spell (B)
1 Litous
☎ 8960676, 8960131/2, 8961868

**SOUNION (SOUNIO): TELEPHONE PREFIX
0292 POST CODE 195 00**
Hotel Egeon (A)
☎ 39200, 39234

Hotel Triton (B)
Athinon-Souniou
☎ 39103, 39316

Hotel Saron (C)
Lavriou-Souniou
☎ 39144

**AEGINA TOWN: TELEPHONE PREFIX
0297 POST CODE 180 10**
Hotel Nerina (B)
21 P. Eginitou
☎ 22795

Hotel Areti (C)
9 N. Kazantzaki
☎ 22806, 23917, 23593

Hotel Avra (C)
2 N. Kazantzaki
☎ 22303, 25036, 23917, 24493, 23968

YOUTH HOSTELS
The Greek Association of Youth
Hostels
4 Dragatsaniou
Athens
☎ (01) 323 4107
Athens Youth Hostel (Ksenon
Neotitos): 1 Aghiou Meletiou &
Kypselis, Kipseli (North of Areos
Park) ☎ (01) 822 5860
International Youth Hostel:
Peoniou 52 Stathmos Larissis ☎ (01)
883 2878

CAMPING
* = Open all year
There are four sites on the outskirts
of Athens offering on-site dining
facilities, bars and shops.

Athens Camping
198 Athinon
☎ (01) 5814101, 5820353

Daphni Camping
Daphni
☎ (01) 5811562/3

Varkiza Beach Camping*
Faskomilia Varkiza
☎ (01) 8973613/4, 8970012

Voula Camping (NTOG)*
A Alipedo Voulas
☎ (01) 8952712, 8953248

Sounio Beach Camping
Half-way between Sounion & Lavrion.
☎ (0292) 39358, 39718, (01) 7233910

Festivals

Athens
Herod Atticus Odeon
Performances during the summer
at 8.30pm and at 9pm in September. Tickets are sold at:
The Athens Festival Office, 4
Stadiou
☎ (01) 3221459/3223111-9 ext 137
Monday-Saturday 8.30am-2pm &
5pm-7pm. Sunday 10am-1pm and
The Herod Atticus Odeon on
performance days 5-9pm.
☎ (01) 3232771 Advance sale of
tickets begins 15 days before each
event.

Lycabettus Theatre
Performances during the summer
at 9pm. Tickets sold at The Athens
Festival Office as above ☎ ext 240
and at the Lycabettus Theatre on
performance days 7-9pm ☎ (01)
7227236. Advance sale of tickets
begins 10 days before each event.

Sound & Light
Athens - Acropolis - Pnyx
April-October. Daily in English
9-9.45pm. Information and tickets
from The Athens Festival Office as
above ☎ ext 127 and at the entrance
to the show.
☎ (01) 9226210

Dora Stratou (Filopappou Hill)
Greek Folk Dance. End May-end
September. Daily 10.15pm.
Wednesday & Sunday 8.15 & 10.15pm.
Information ☎ (01) 3244395/9214650

Tourist Information Centres

Greek National Tourist Offices
(EOT) Information desks:

Athens
The East Airport
☎ 969 9500

2 Karageorgi Servias Street
Syntagma
Athens (National Bank of Greece
   building.)
☎ 322 2545

Syntagma Square & 1 Ermou Street
Athens
☎ 325 2267/8

Directorate of Tourism of East
Mainland Greece and the Islands
Marina Zeas
Port of Piraeus
☎ 413 5716/413 5730/413 4709

EOT provide a very good street
plan free of Athens centre and
Piraeus, which includes transport
information, combined with a plan
of the Arterial routes in Athens and
an Attica map. Information sheets
are available for: Accommodation;
Bus, Train and Air Services; Bus
Timetable; Ferry
Timetable; Car Storage Garages in
Athens & Piraeus.

2

CORINTH AND THE ARGOLID

Here in the Argolid, the heartland of the ancient Mycenaeans, lies the most remarkable record of human culture and achievement. Nowhere else in Greece is there such a concentration of archaeological sites all of which demand to be visited. Tiryns, Epidauros, Mycenae, Corinth, Acrocorinth and Ancient Nemea all lie within relatively close proximity. It may sound like an intensive culture trail but to make it feel more like a holiday there are some excellent coastal resorts on hand in Nafplio, Tolon and Paleo Epidauros, which make ideal bases for exploring the region. The Saronic Gulf islands of Poros, Hydra and Spetse are all within easy reach and they make a welcome diversion when cultural overload threatens.

Nafplio, at the southern end of the Argolid, crowned by the Palimidi fortress and graced by the Bourdzi fort on the offshore islet, has a lively air and plenty of character. If a beach is a priority then nearby Tolon scores highly. Primarily a fishing village, Tolon now ribbons its way along the coast. Many of the hotels are sandwiched between the road and the sea so that they open directly onto the beach at the rear. Justly popular, Tolon is crowded in high season. Paleo Epidauros is ideal for those seeking a little more peace. Beautifully situated in a picturesque bay, it retains all the character of a fishing village while coping with its role in tourism. The tours described here are based from Nafplio but they can be just as easily enjoyed from any of these bases.

Tour 1 • South To The Peloponnese (140km/87 miles)

Mainly over good roads, this journey is comfortably achieved in half a day leaving time to accommodate a visit to Mycenae, one of the few sites open for the full day. The road out of Athens passes by the

Daphni Monastery and close to Elefsina providing a convenient opportunity to see them if they have not already been visited. Both are detailed in Chapter 1.

Escaping Athens is not especially easy but the road out to Corinth is signposted from Omonia Square. Suburbs seem to stretch on interminably and only after Elefsina, on 28km (17 miles), does it feel as though Athens has finally been left behind. Soon after Elefsina, toll booths announce the start of 'motorway.' Do not expect any significant road improvement and beware of the variable number of traffic lanes, sometimes down to one. The motorway ends with unused 'toll check' booths as Corinth is reached in 80km (50 miles). Keep to the left lane at the approach of the booths to be in position for crossing the almost insignificant bridge over the canal. A large parking area on the right with restaurant, shop and fast food caters for the passing tourists. A short walk back provides an opportunity to look along the 6km (4 mile) long canal. Started by the silver spade of Nero, it took longer than most projects and was eventually completed in 1890. It became instrumental in Piraeus developing into a major port but, at only 25m (82ft) wide, its usefulness soon became limited. One of the modern liners inching its way through is a spectacle which never fails to draw the crowds.

Follow Tripoli signs initially from Corinth but be careful to watch out for the Argos/Nafplio signs on reaching Acrocorinth. The road flirts with the railway, constantly bumpily crossing and recrossing. Rolling hills give way to the Argive plain with southerly progress, to shimmering silver green leaves of the olives and the scarlet splash of poppy fields. Mycenae (Mikines) is not too clearly signed so be alert for a left turn on reaching the village of Fychtia. The site, set on a hill with a mountain backdrop, is 2km (1 mile) further on through the village of **Mikines**.

It is generally thought the people who developed the Mycenaean culture around 1550BC were warrior-like Indo-Europeans who entered Greece from the Balkans or southern Russia. Their culture, inspired by the Minoans, flourished from 1550 to 1200BC and spread its influence throughout the Peloponnese, into the mainland and the Aegean. They built citadels with walls up to 6m (20ft) thick using huge rocks, 'cyclopean' walls as they were later called because the peasants believed that only Cyclops could have placed the stones in position. Within the citadels were built the Royal dwellings occupied by the king who was also the priest and general leader and by a hierarchy of officials. By 1500BC, towards the height of their domination, there were at least 320 citadels under their rule.

The search for knowledge of this golden age has more than a touch of romance about it. Apart from the archaeological work and pottery finds which tell much about the culture, later writings have also been significant. This is especially true of Homer's epic poems, *The Iliad* and *The Odyssey*, which were believed to have originated much later, around the ninth century or eighth century BC. Although rich in myth and legend, they seem to have a core of historical fact, *The Iliad* relates the tale of how King Agamemnon, overlord of Archaea (Greece), master of 'well-built Mycenae,' together with his brother Menelaus led their forces against King Priam of Troy. This was because Paris, one of Priam's sons had run away with the beautiful Helen of Argos, wife of Menelaus. After a protracted but victorious war, Agamemnon returned to find that his wife, Clytemnestra, had taken Aegisthos as a lover. Conspiring together, they brought Agamemnon to a rather undignified end, by murdering him whilst in his bath.

Mycenae passed into historical oblivion for centuries until Heinrich Schliemann, an amateur archaeologist from Germany came onto the scene. Inspired by the Homeric tales, especially the references to 'Mycenae ... a town rich in gold,' Heinrich Schliemann started excavations in 1876. After only 6 weeks he discovered a grave circle crammed with golden objects including funeral masks. On 28 November 1876, Schliemann sent his now famous telegraph to King George I of the Hellenes in which he claimed 'I have gazed upon the face of Agamemnon.' The gold mask, which he believed to be Agamemnon and which is now housed in the National Museum in Athens, was later established as belonging to an earlier period. One of the irresistible pleasures of a visit to Mycenae lies in trying to fit the Homeric tales with what you see before you.

A violent earthquake around 1250BC, the time of its greatest prosperity, brought about some partial rebuilding only to be further devastated by fire some 50 years later. Further fires led to the decline and fall of the Mycenaean civilisation around 1100-1050BC. The main points of interest:

The Lion Gate: This famous gateway takes its name from the triangular-shaped sculpture above the door lintel depicting two lions either side of a Minoan column. This triangular symbol of power is believed to have a practical purpose in protecting the lintel from the weight of the wall. A relieving triangle is also seen at the entrance to the Treasury of Atreus. The Lion Gate forms the entrance to the site proper.

Grave Circle A: This is the Royal cemetery uncovered by Schliemann in 1876 were he found burial furnishings which proved to be the richest treasure in the history of Greek archaeology.

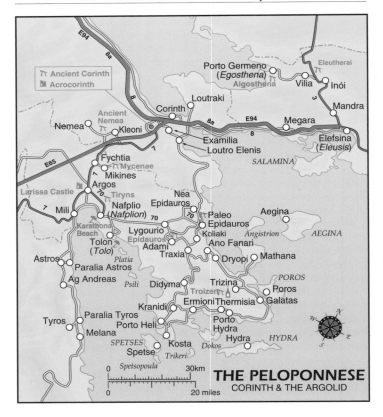

THE PELOPONNESE
CORINTH & THE ARGOLID

Amongst the gold cups, gold crowns and inlaid swords were four gold death masks, one of which he believed belonged to Agamemnon. Now dated as sixteenth century with the last internment around fifteenth century BC, it is centuries earlier than the Trojan Wars and dispels Schliemann's unshakeable belief that he had discovered the grave of all those murdered by Aegisthos on their return from Ilium.

The circle is formed by a double ring of dressed slabs which are thought to have been filled with rubble while the top was covered by horizontal slabs. Within this six graves shafts were hewn down into the rock to various levels, five were discovered by Schliemann and the sixth was discovered more recently near the entrance.

The Palace: Located on the summit of the acropolis, there are now

The walls of the Palimidi fortress crown the hill at Nafplio

Now over a century old, the Corinth Canal is too narrow for most modern liners

only foundations to help visualise the dimensions. The entrance from the north leads through two guard rooms to the Propylon were the column bases can be seen. Centrally situated is the Great Court. A porch and a vestibule led east into the Megaron, the central room of the palace. Centrally placed here is the sacred Hearth marked now by a ring of stones while the King's throne stood at the centre of the south wall. Still to be seen are the bases for the four wooden pillars which supported the roof. There are remains of a temple dedicated to Athena on the summit from a later period, around the sixth century BC.

The Cult Centre: This is the name given to the group of buildings to the south of Grave Circle A which were built in the thirteenth century BC. Discoveries in these recent excavations suggest a temple and shrines where religious activity took place. The many finds include realistically modelled clay snakes which form a link with Minoan religious practice.

The Secret Cistern: This lies at the eastern side of the site. Steps lead down in total darkness to a deep underground spring. A good torch and considerable care is needed to see it.

The Treasury of Atreus (The Tomb of Agamemnon): This lies outside the main site alongside the approach road. It is one of the finest and best preserved Tholos tombs found in Greece, and one of the latest, built around 1350BC. The connection with Atreus, father of Agamemnon, or Agamemnon is speculative. Unlike the grave shafts, these tombs had all been plundered so less in known about their use but finds of skeletons in other tholoi indicate burial tombs.

There are several more tombs scattered around outside the acropolis site, none of which offer much to the casual visitor. The best known are Grave Circle B, to the right of the road opposite the parking area and the Tomb of Clytemnestra on the right of the approach to the Lion Gate. After returning to the main road, Nafplio lies only a further 25km (15½ miles) to the south with only Argos to negotiate.

❋ **Nafplio** (Nafplion), capital of the Argolid, is claimed by the locals to be the loveliest town in all Greece. Looking out over the fort of Bourdzi on the tiny offshore island and beyond into the Argolic Gulf, towered over by the Venetian fortress of Palimidi, its position alone gives credence to this belief. Add another castle complex in Acronafplio, a ramble of narrow, sometimes stepped streets, stuccoed houses, wooden balconies cascading with flowers, Turkish mosques, traditional tavernas in plenty and it is enough to convince visitors that it is quite incomparable.

Known from the Mycenaean era as a naval base for Argos, Nafplio has suffered a somewhat turbulent passage through time. Valuable as a trading post, it was twice in the hands of the Venetians, first time when it was bought in 1388 and the second time when it was recovered from the Turks in 1686 by Count Konigsmark, a lieutenant under the famous Morisini. The Palimidi Fortress, built 1711-14 by the Venetians and named after the mythical Palamedes, son of Poseidon and inventor of lighthouses and dice amongst other things, failed to keep the Turks at bay. Nafplio fell to them in 1715. Under the command of Kolokotronis, Greek forces besieged Nafplio in the War of Independence in 1821-1822 and brought the Turkish garrison to near starvation. Finally captured, Nafplio became the focal point of Greek opposition to the Turks.

From 1829 until 1834, Nafplio assumed the role of the first capital of the new Greek state and the Corfiot, John Kapodistrias, Greece's first regent. The fierce and sometimes violent factionalism was a major problem after the war and Kapodistrias fell a victim in his efforts to quell it. He was assassinated in Nafplio in 1831. Fear of civil war led the Great Powers to intervene. Believing the way forward was for Greece to become a monarchy, Britain, France and Russia approached King Ludwig I of Bavaria who agreed for his son Otto to accept the crown. The monarchy was ratified in Nafplio's suburb of Pronoia in May 1832. Proud of its role in this period of history, the names of kings, queens, war heroes and political leaders are scattered freely amongst Nafplio's streets, avenues and platias.

Either the new road up to **Palimidi Fortress** is a well kept secret or people prefer the challenge of climbing the 900 or so steps to reach it. The pay box is at the top. Having expended the energy to climb up, none is dissuaded from entering on account of the small charge. This remarkably well preserved fortress is entered by a series of gates bearing the Lion of St Mark. There is still plenty of footwork to do if you plan to explore the three independent fortresses inside and enjoy the views from the 215m (705ft) summit, especially the bird's eye view down over Nafplio.

Exploration of Acronafplio, also known as Its Kale, is less demanding and, since it is now occupied by the Xenia hotel complex, less enticing. Its Kale is a corruption of the Turkish name 'UÇ Kale' meaning three castles (Greek, Frankish and Venetian). A fortress from ancient times, there has been successive rebuilding over the years. The lower castle, Castelo del Torrione, now housing the Xenia hotel, was designed by Gambello as was the castle standing on Bourdzi Isle. The luxury class Xenia's Palace now occupies the upper castle providing its residents with a superb view down over Bourdzi and the whole sweep of the bay.

The deep blue waters at Nafplio town beach

Grave Circle A at Mycenae where Schliemann believed he had found the gold death mask of Agamemnon

Walking To Karathona Beach

The small Ellinikós Organismós Tourismoú (National Tourism Organisation of Greece or EOT) pay beach in Naplio becomes rather crowded at times. For those prepared to stretch a leg there is a large although narrow sandy beach about 3km (2 miles) away. A solitary taverna apart, do not expect facilities. It is a traffic free route although the odd rogue motor-cyclist can be expected.

Set out from the town beach heading south with the sea on your right. Follow the pedestrian track along the coast and watch out for some interesting flowers, especially where the hills on the left decline to scrubland. Spring walkers can expect to find wild orchids such as the mirror orchid (*Ophrys speculum*), the pyramidal orchid (*Anacamptis pyramidalis*) and the tongue orchid (*Serapias parviflora*).

The beach is reached after some 40 to 45 minutes.

A panoramic view from the Palimidi Fortress, Nafplio

Nafplio is not all chasing up hills, the lower town too is worthy of exploration. The main square, Platea Syndagmatos, bordered by three Turkish mosques, is a good starting point. One mosque is now a cinema, another has been reconsecrated and converted into a church, Ag Georgios, and the third, in the south-west corner, has the distinction of being the first parliament building for the newly independent Greece. The Archaeological Museum at the west end of the square houses many artefacts of the Mycenaean period including some intriguing jointed clay figures. The Folk Art Museum, tucked away in Ipsiladou street, is also worth a visit.

Tour 2 • Historic Argolid (195km/121 miles)

This tour, generally over good roads, fits comfortably into 2 days. It is not the distance which absorbs the time but the number of sites to accommodate before the mid-afternoon closing time. Paleo Epidauros makes an ideal stop-over.

Only 4km (2 miles) outside Nafplio on the road to Argos, **Tiryns** is quickly reached. Masonry falls in the early spring of 1992 were serious enough for the authorities to judge that the site was unsafe for visitors until a survey and restorative work had been completed. Although assurances were given that it would re-open, they were unable to say how long it would remain closed.

Although its inland position on a small hummock seems insignificant, in Mycenaean times it stood as an impressive citadel by the seashore. This fortress-palace, in the style of Mycenae, is enclosed by huge, thick walls now far less than their estimated 20m (66ft) in height. 'Wall-girt Tiryns' was Homers description in *The Iliad* while the Roman travel writer Pausanias, second century AD, compared the walls of Tiryns with the pyramids of Egypt. Inhabited from the Bronze Age, the site was built to its present form during the thirteenth century BC but despite its size and wealth, it never reached the eminence of Mycenae. There is no need to leave your chariot outside because the steep entrance ramp is wide enough to take it but watch out for the nasty turn at the top. Inside, the whole palace complex is one of great architectural skill.

As with Mycenae, the Megaron (Great Hall), with its circular clay hearth, lies at the heart but its best known features are the vaulted galleries and secret passages. Many of the apartments were richly decorated with wall frescos and painted floors.

Larissa Castle at **Argos** is a prominent landmark seen long before Argos is entered. Reaching it is less easy. Head past the main square and look for the insignificant 'Kastro' sign indicating the road out to the north-west and a similar sign indicating a left turn further on. There is plenty of car parking space outside the castle entrance. It is an unattended site with no entry charge.

Archaeologists found evidence of Mycenaean occupation in excavations at Larissa Castle but it is the Byzantines, Franks, Venetians and Turks who have contributed to its present form. The extensive views from the castle take in the Argolic Gulf and much of the Argolid on a clear day.

Argos was important in ancient times but the prosperous modern town of Argos swamps the old site. The excavated remains, such as they are, are not too rewarding to the casual visitor. The best place to catch a glimpse of the past history is at the fine and airy museum located south-west of but close to the main square, attractive with its sidewalk cafés. Well displayed, the artefacts include bronze objects, pottery from the Mycenaean period and later work from the Roman period.

It is back to bumping over railway lines on the road north from Argos but is unlikely to distract from the heady scent of orange blossom which fills the lower plains throughout the early spring months. Once beyond Fychtia, watch out for the sign left to Nemea; the ancient site is before the village of the same name.

With so much to see in the Argolid, **Nemea** is not really part of the main tourist trail and it receives less attention than it would if it were in some other part of Greece. Located in a delightful valley famous for its red wine, Nemea has its special place in history. Near here Heracles (the Roman Hercules) slew the Nemean lion with his bare hands, the first of his twelve labours. Nemea was not an ancient city but, like Olympia, was a sanctuary with a temple dedicated to Zeus. It too held biennial panhellenic athletic games started, according to one legend, by Heracles after he had slain the lion. The prize to the victors was nothing more than a crown of wild parsley.

A visit to the excellent on site museum is strongly recommended before the site is explored. Apart from the various finds from this and nearby locations, there is a useful model which shows the layout of the site. The Temple of Nemean Zeus from 340-320BC, now with only three of its Doric columns standing, is the most obvious building but south of that are foundations of the treasury buildings and the bath house.

Return to the main road through the village of Kleoni and continue north through undulating hills to Ancient Corinth which is off left soon after joining the Corinth-Tripoli road.

Occupied from before Mycenaean times, **Ancient Corinth** did not rise to significance until around the eighth century BC. It was rebuilt by the Dorians to take advantage of its strategic position where a road allowed ships to be dragged on rollers between the Gulf of Corinth and the Saronic Gulf. From around 657BC for the next century, a succession of tyrant leaders, Kypselos, his son Periander and his nephew Psammetichos, threw their efforts into expanding trade and commerce. Corinth rapidly became a mercantile power spreading its influence throughout the Mediterranean, east and west. Its population rose as high as 30,000 in its most flourishing period as it enjoyed the prosperity gained from its unique trading position. A colonisation programme to relieve the problems of feeding such a vast population founded cities on Corfu (Korkyra) and Sicily (Syracuse) which themselves became influential.

In this climate of prosperity the Isthmian Games were started which achieved a prestige second only to the Olympics and the arts too flourished. The decline of Corinth started in the fifth century BC with Athens increasingly taking a share of their markets. Wars too had their effect and both the Peloponnesian War (431-404BC) and the Corinthian War (395-7BC) left them weaker. Prosperity returned again in a period of Macedonian rule which started in 338BC and ended in 224BC when the garrison was expelled. Corinth became the seat of the revised Achaean League and remained a lively trading centre until the arrival of the Romans.

Larissa Castle is a prominent landmark overlooking Argos

The Corinthians were well known for their pursuit of pleasure. As worshippers of Aphrodite, the goddess of love, the licentious activities of these ancients reached new heights of profligacy. Prostitutes numbered in thousands rather than hundreds. All levels of society were catered for but the most illustrious of the courtesans, and history records Lois as one of the most sought after, were well educated and well schooled in all the necessary arts. A temple dedicated to Aphrodite was built on Acrocorinth, the prominent hill south of Ancient Corinth.

After the defeat of the Achaean League by the Romans in 146BC, the ancient city was razed to the ground by Mummius. It remained that way until Julius Caesar planted a colony there in 44BC. Rebuilt in Roman style, it quickly rose to importance as capital of the province of Greece. Wealth returned as did its reputation for prostitution which brought the Apostle Paul 'in fear and trembling' to convert the pagans.

It survived ravages by Herulian forces in AD267 and later by Alaric forces in AD395 but not the earthquakes of AD522 and AD551. It recovered something of its prosperity in the eleventh century only to suffer domination by a succession of captors. The earthquakes of 1858 again devastated the town and brought about relocation to its present position.

One of the many archaeological remains to be seen at the ancient site of Corinth

For one of the largest and most complex archaeological sites in Greece, Ancient Corinth disappoints from the poor on site information. Most of the remains on view are from the Roman period with just a touch of the original Greek city to be seen. After so many earthquakes it is not surprising that there is so little standing yet equally remarkable is that the foundations are so well preserved. The ruins are spread over a large area, not all of them within the enclosed site. The main points of interest:

The Odeon: This is outside the main site, just across the road from the entrance. It was constructed by the Romans to hold around 3,000 people.

The Theatre: Just north of the Odeon but not much to see. Built sometime in the fifth century BC and rebuilt by the Romans. Within the enclosure is:

The Museum: Exhibits include a good many artefacts from both the Greek and Roman periods.

The Temple of Apollo: With seven Doric columns still standing, this is one of the more prominent monuments on the site and undeniably Greek. Built in the sixth century BC when Corinth was growing in power and wealth, this is possibly one of the oldest temples in Greece.

The Agora: The market or meeting place. To the side were shops thought to be places of refreshment from the number of bones, both fish and animal, and cups found.

Fountain of Peirene: One of two natural springs, the other is on the acropolis. The water was stored in reservoirs hidden by a fountain house with a six-arched façade and fed into a sunken pool which is now dry.

Lechaion Street: Running to the northern port, part of this wide, paved road, flanked by colonnades backed by shops, has now been exposed.

For **Acrocorinth** continue past the site and take the signed road on the left. The fountain of Hadji Mustafa is passed on the final wind up the hill. There is plenty of parking space by the café. It is an unguarded site with no entry fee. Looking down on the main site from a height of 575m (1,886ft), the acropolis of Acrocorinth may tell little of its early Greek history but it does offer excellent views encompassing the Gulf of Corinth and the Saronic Gulf as well as a chance to look down over the ground plan of Ancient Corinth. Guarding the gateway to the Peloponnese, this important citadel has been captured and recaptured, built and rebuilt throughout the ages. The extensive towered walls guarding the hill top are Byzantine with contributions from the Franks, Venetians and the Turks. Three entrance gateways tell this story. The first is largely Turkish, the second Frankish rebuilt by the Venetians and the inner one originally fourth century BC. Once inside, pathways over rough ground lead through the herbage to the various points of interest. There are ruins of Turkish houses and Turkish barracks, Byzantine chapels and cisterns some seriously threatened by the undergrowth. The upper Peirene spring lies in the the south-east corner near the barracks but is not easily found. The highest summit housed the Temple of Aphrodite which was served in its day by a thousand religious prostitutes. It is hard to evoke memories of it now for this site has in turn been a church, a watch tower, a mosque and a paved viewpoint. It is the latter which makes it worth the climb.

Return to the main Athens road and, if the changed road priorities allow after current road-works, look to continue across to head for Examilia and the coast. Otherwise turn north and pick up the next road to Examilia. Slightly elevated, the scenic coastal road winds and twists its way south around hills cloaked in pine or through groves of almonds or olive occasionally yielding glimpses of the seashore. A sign warns of 'Continuous Dangerous Bents' (*sic*) but equally dangerous are the wandering goats and sheep. A left turn leads into Paleo Epidauros.

Strung thinly around an almost enclosed bay backed by pine clad mountains, a first glimpse of **Paleo Epidauros** suggests a slight air of ❈ neglect as if still awaiting discovery and not really expecting visitors. Once down amongst the colourful fishing boats watching the fishermen working on their nets, its divided role comes into perspective and the charm of its location overwhelms. The tavernas, like the hotels, mostly look out onto fishing boats dotted about on Homer's 'wine-dark sea.' The village is a staging post for ancient Epidauros and had the same role in antiquity. It sees a fair passing trade, especially throughout the festival of ancient Greek drama in summer when Athenians arrive on excursion boats from Piraeus, just a 2-hour sail away.

Paleo Epidauros has a recently discovered ancient theatre of its ᴨ own which is quite a gem and not yet on the tourist map. It lies on the headland to the right and takes around 10 to 15 minutes walking to reach it. Follow the bay round onto the promontory until the track on the right opposite the church is reached. A sign on the eucalyptus tree directs to 'Cocktail, Playhouse Bar.' The track leads gently uphill through orange groves to reach a T-junction. Continue by turning right (a left turn takes you to some other excavations on the headland) and follow the track around to reach a shuttered stone house shaded by a palm tree. Go up the track on the left and the theatre is

Wild muscari surround the magnificent Epidauros theatre, famed for its splendid acoustics

on the right, literally in the garden of the stone house. Easily visible through the wire fence, a good view is obtained by following around the perimeter to the rear of the theatre. Much of the tiered stone seating is still in place and particularly impressive is the well preserved inner circle of seats for the dignitaries.

Leave Paleo Epidauros to the south and follow the 'Galatas' sign left at the first junction. This new road reveals magnificent views as it winds and climbs away from Paleo Epidauros to join the main Epidauros road some 13km (8 miles) later; turn right. Once through the village of Adami, the mountain landscape imposes a fierce but transient beauty which is lost to a calm gentility before Epidauros is reached.

Epidauros was dedicated to Asklepios, the god of healing and
ranked highly amongst the many such sanctuaries scattered
throughout Greece. Originally, Apollo was worshipped here as the
healing god but by the fourth century BC he had been replaced by his
son Asklepios. According to myth, Asklepios, the son of Apollo and
the earthling Kronos, was reared by the centaur Chiron who
schooled him in the arts of healing. In turn he passed on his knowledge and skills to his daughters Panacaea and Hygeia who became
part of the cult. Epidauros received pilgrims constantly and belief in
the healing powers of this sanctuary lasted for almost a thousand
years.

Although Epidauros is a fairly extensive site, much of it is only
excavated foundations and a number of those roped off. The interest
for most centres on the magnificent and well preserved theatre built
to seat around 14,000. It is especially famed for its splendid acoustics
and the visitor need only sit quietly somewhere on the upper seating
and await the vocal demonstrations from the more extrovert tourists.
Built in the fourth century BC, it seems to have had little restoration
until modern times. Now it is used for the summer festival of ancient
Greek drama.

The Temple of Asklepios lies just north of the Roman Odeon and
the round building here, the Tholos, excites considerable curiosity

The fishing harbour at Tolon

and speculation. It was built over a labyrinth of concentric stone circles with access via a trap door. One theory amongst others is that it was used to house the sacred snakes. A model depicting how it might have looked is contained in the museum.

Perhaps the first port of call should be the museum which is located just inside the entrance to the site. Lygourio is the only village of any size passed on the route back to Nafplio but, unless fuel or refreshments are required, there seems no reason to stop. The remaining 24km (15 miles) is a peaceful run through quiet country-side.

Tour 3 • Off The Beaten Track Argolid (216km/134 miles)

Even allowing a couple of hours on the island of Poros, this tour through the countryside of the Argolid requires only one day. Further time is needed if Hydra and Spetse are to be included.

Tolon (Tolo) lies only 13km (8 miles) away from Nafplio and is well signposted. On the final approach, the road forks and both are signposted for Tolon centre but the right fork is the more direct. Follow the road as it winds endlessly through the village until the port area with space for parking is reached.

Bounded by low hills, Tolon fits comfortably around a long sweep of sandy bay looking onto a small island. A line of hotels with a scattering of tavernas front directly onto the narrow beach. The northern end of the beach, away from the port and the main town, has finer sand and is less public.

Return from Tolon to the Nafplio-Lygourio road and continue along mainly good roads towards Galatas. The route takes you through quiet countryside, past Epidauros and through Adami. Villages along the route are often nothing more than a cluster of houses and usually difficult to identify with the names on the map. Olives which are a near constant part of the modern landscape are known from Mycenaean times, carbonised traces of olives were found on Mycenaean palace sites, but the wide scale farming of olives is believed to have developed some centuries later. After a left turn at Traxia, the road winds and twists through undulating coun-tryside revealing small areas of cultivated farmland snatched from the grip of the barren hills. The sight of Ano Fanari clinging to the rocky hillside signifies the start of a descent towards a scenic run along the coast. After leaving the coast, oranges and lemons in luxurious growth tell of a fertile region which was once Troizenia in ancient times. The modern village of Trizina is signposted off to the left and near the village, scattered over a wide area, are the remains of ancient Troizen. **Poros**, lying just offshore here, draws even closer as Galatas is reached.

Car ferries and water taxis ply back and forward frequently. The fare for passengers is cheap by any standards. Those intent on seeing the monastery of Zoodochou Pigis, a 6½ km (4 miles) drive out of town, might consider taking a car over otherwise it is barely necessary, Poros has only narrow streets and the island a limited road network. With its close proximity to Athens and regular ferry connection, weekends and high season sees the island fairly busy with local trade. Add to this a good dash of international tourism and it adds up to a busy scene. The waterfront with its cafés, tavernas and tourist shops is invariably bustling but the narrow streets which lead up the steep hill into the town provide a quick escape route for those who like to browse in peace. The clock tower is a good focal point to enjoy the views. It is only a short walk out of town to the east to reach the canal bridge which connects the small volcanic island of Sphaeria to the larger wooded Kalauria which together are Poros. The island is short on beaches but the best lies at Kanali, to the right after crossing the canal bridge.

Back on the mainland, **Galatas** has little to offer apart from waterside cafés looking over the narrow straits to Poros town. The route south-east out of Galatas passes shortly through the lemon forests of Limonodasos with its estimated 30,000 lemon trees although the carnations which are also grown commercially in the region are more eye-catching. The road, surfaced and wide enough for two way traffic, wends along the coastline passing through isolated clusters of housing which are difficult to identify with place names on a map. Lemon groves persist until the first significant village, Thermisia, just after the holiday enclosure of Porto Hydra. **Ermioni**, 11km (7 miles) further on, still remarkably free from tourist developments has ferry services to both Hydra and Spetse during the summer months but the more regular route to Spetse is from Kosta at the southern end of the peninsula. Pastoral scenery predominates through Kranidi to Didyma. Once beyond, the road winds and climbs through mountains until the outward route is rejoined at Traxia.

Spetse And Hydra

From early April onwards throughout the summer, excursion boats depart Tolon daily to the islands of Spetse and Hydra, usually as a combined trip. Hydra, reached after a 3-hour sail, has a picturesque and bustling harbour crowded with fishing boats and lined with waterside tavernas and pavement cafés. The island has no roads suitable for motor vehicles so transport is by mule and pack horse and they too are part of the harbour scene. It is a town of narrow streets, pastel coloured red-roofed houses tiered up the enclosing hills and donkey droppings. Once the town itself has been explored, it is easy to wander out into the hills along the many mule tracks.

It is perhaps a little unfortunate that Spetse is usually the second port of call since its harbour is less atmospheric than Hydra although it is not without its own charm. Normally it is a shorter stop leaving time only for a brief exploration of the fine old houses in the town. Like Hydra, there is no beach immediately to hand.

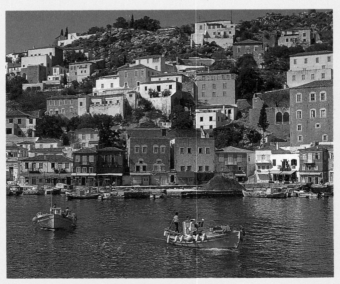

The island of Hydra has a picturesque harbour

Island hopping in the fast lane... by hydrofoil

The peaceful island of Hydra is a welcomed diversion from sightseeing

Additional Information

Places to Visit

Ancient Corinth
Site and Museum
Open: 8.30am-2.45pm daily
including Sundays and holidays.

Acrocorinth Castle
Unattended site and open at all times.

Argos
Museum
Open: daily 8.30am-3pm including
Sundays and holidays but closed
on Mondays.

Larissa Castle
Unattended site and open at all times.

Epidauros
Site and Museum
Open: 8am-5pm weekdays and
8.30am-3pm Saturday and Sunday.

Mycenae
Open: 8am-7pm weekdays and
8.30am-3pm on Saturday, Sunday
and holidays.

Nafplio
Archaeological Museum
Open: daily 8.30am-3pm including
weekends but closed on Monday.

Palamidi Fortress
Open: weekdays 8am-4pm and
8.30am- 2.30pm on Saturday and
Sunday.

Nemea
Site and Museum
Open: weekdays 8.45am-3pm and
9.30am-2.30pm on Sundays and
holidays. Closed on Mondays.

Accommodation

HOTELS
* = Open all year
Hotels from luxury (L) down to C
class are listed but rooms are also
available, especially in the larger
resorts like Nafplio.

NAFPLIO: TELEPHONE PREFIX 0752
*Xenia Palace** (L)
Hotel and bungalows
Akronafplia ☎ 28981/3

*Xenia** (A)
Akronaplia ☎ 28991/3

*Hotel Amphitryon** (A)
Staikopolou ☎ 27366

*Hotel Agamemnon** (B)
Akti Miaouli ☎ 28021

*Hotel Victoria** (C)
Staikopoulou ☎ 27420

*Hotel Elena** (C)
Sid Merarchias ☎ 23217

*Hotel Nafplia** (C)
Navarinou ☎ 28167

*Hotel Park** (C)
Dervenakion ☎ 27428

TOLON: TELEPHONE PREFIX 0752
*Hotel Dolphin** (B) ☎ 59162/220
Hotel Sofia (B) ☎ 59567/8
Hotel Aris (C) ☎ 59231/510
Hotel Artemis (C) ☎ 59458/125
Hotel Assini Beach (C) ☎ 59347
Hotel Christina (C) ☎ 59001
Hotel Elena's (C) ☎ 59158
Hotel Flisvos (C) ☎ 59223/437
Hotel Knossos (C) ☎ 59174
Hotel Minoa (C) ☎ 59207/146

PALEO EPIDAUROS: TELEPHONE PREFIX 0753
Marialena* (B) Furnished Apartments.
☎ 41090
Hotel Aegeon* (C) ☎ 41381
Hotel Aktis (C) ☎ 41407
Hotel Apollon (C) ☎ 41295
Hotel Christina* (C) ☎ 41451
Hotel Hellas(C) ☎ 41226
Hotel Maik* (C) ☎ 41213
Hotel Maronika (C) ☎ 41391/41491
Hotel Paola Beach (C) ☎ 41397
Hotel Plaza (C) ☎ 41395
Hotel Poseidon* (C) ☎ 41211
Hotel Rena (C) ☎ 41311
Hotel Saronis (C) ☎ 41514
Verdelis Inn (C) ☎ 41332

NEA EPIDAUROS: TELEPHONE PREFIX 0753
Hotel Epidauros* (C) ☎ 31209

Mykines: TELEPHONE PREFIX 0751
Hotel La Petite Planete* (B)
Hristou Tsounta ☎ 66240

Hotel Agamemnon* (C)
3 Hristou Tsounta ☎ 66222/32

ERMIONI: TELEPHONE PREFIX 0754
Hotel Lena-Mary (B) ☎ 31450/1

CAMPING

* = Open all year
There are some thirty-nine official
camp sites scattered around the
Argolid. Most offer on-site dining
facilities, bars and shops.

Kineta Corinthias
Assini*
☎ 0296 62005

Mycenae
Mycenae
☎ 0751 66247

Paleo Epidauros
Bekas Camping
☎ 0753 41333/394/583

Plaka Drepanou
Alkyon
☎ 0752 92336/01, 9815929

Nafplio
Lefka
☎ 0752 92394

Nea Epidauros
Diamantis
☎ 0753 31293/31240

Tolon
Avra
☎ 0752 59085/520

Lido I
☎ 0752 59489

Sunset
☎ 0752 59566

Sfakes Tolou
Lido II
☎ 0752 59396

Tourist Information Centre

Nafplio
Municipality Information Office
Iatrou Square
☎ 0752 24444
Hotel list available covering Nafplio,
Argos, Tolon and Drepano.
Local Transport: three buses daily
connect Nafplio to Mycenae and
four to Epidauros. Tolon is served
by an hourly service and there is a
regular schedule for Athens and
Argos.

3

LACONIA

Tucked away in the south-east corner of the Peloponnese, the
province of Laconia is scenically enriched by two parallel mountain ranges. The Parnon which climbs to a mighty 1,935m (6,347ft) in
the north of the province declines to a rumbling spine as it runs into
the Laconian peninsula, the setting for Monemvasia. Further to the
south-west, and topping 2,400m (7,872ft), the majestic Taygetos
(Taigetos) runs down into the central peninsula, the Mani. Between
the two ranges lies the fertile Eurotas plain, the garden of Sparta.
Against this backdrop of snow-capped mountain peaks, precipitous
rock faces, deep ravines and lush green forests is another distinct
chapter of Greek history, written not in the intangible mists of the
ancient past but in the more solid and recent medieval times. Mistra,
sprawling against the foothills of the Taygetos and crowned by a
castle, once a vibrant intellectual power in the Byzantine empire and
rich on silk now lies dead and deserted. In such a picturesque setting
and overrun with wild flowers, Mistra is one of the most exciting
sites in the Peloponnese although the devotees of Monemvasia
might take exception to praising it too highly. The old town of
Monemvasia sits on a rocky peninsula, now an island since the
isthmus was cut centuries ago to fortify its defences. Handily situated for sea contact with Constantinople, it was the home of the
governor of the Peloponnese in Byzantine times until Mistra grew in
power. Now it is an atmospheric old town accessible only on foot and
steadily undergoing restoration in its original style.

There is still one more region which is equally compelling, the
Mani. Dusty, dry, barren, rocky Mani occupies the central peninsula
in the south of the Peloponnese and even though it shares the
dwindling spine of the Taygetos, scenically it has little in common
with the rest of the region. Without firm boundaries, the region south

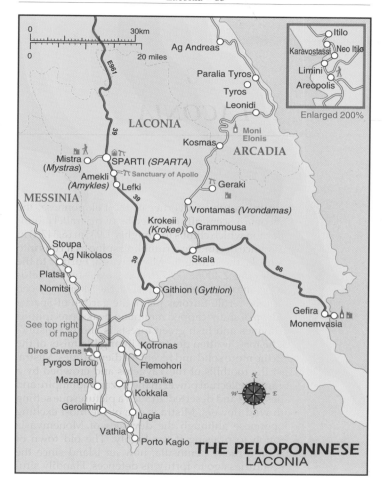

THE PELOPONNESE
LACONIA

of Areopolis is often referred to as inner or deep Mani and the rest to outer Mani. The interest in the Mani lies in its architecture, villages of square, ruggedly built tower houses, its people and their interaction with a barren and hostile environment. History relates how these proud and independent people indulged in insurrections against authority, lawlessness and almost perpetual feuding. A little knowledge of the character of these people turns a tour of deep Mani from a visual to an emotional experience.

Tour 1 • South To Monemvasia (200km/124 miles)

Despite crossing the Parnon range, the journey from Nafplio takes only around 5 hours which leaves time to loiter along the way. Although it is wise to start with a full tank, fuel is available at the larger villages along the route.

After following around the bay, the road south from Nafplio joins the main Argos-Tripoli road at Myli but only briefly. As the main road swings inland, turn left following signs to Astros. Hemmed in by mountains, the road has little option but to follow the coastline squeezing its way tightly between the mountains and the sea in places. The drab scrub covered hills are brightened considerably in spring by the yellow-flowered brooms. Both Astros and the larger Ag Andreas lie a little inland but once beyond the road returns to hug the scenic coastline.

Leonidi, a fairly large town on the estuary of the river Dafno with fuel, shops and telephones, makes absolutely no concession to the through traffic which is forced to thread itself through the narrow streets. Be warned, it can be slow if heavies are involved. Once through it is scenery of a quite different order as the road ascends a long, long gully up into the Parnon mountains. Above, to the left, Moni Elonis appears clinging impossibly to the rocks and, soon after it is spotted, the entrance is signed off left. Still on an upward wind, the highest point of 1,200m (3,936ft) is reached near the village of Kosmas. There are flowers on view for much of the summer at these altitudes and April may be rewarded with *Anemone blanda, Aubrieta gracilis, Muscari* and a small, yellow Gagea species.

The road narrows appreciably as you wind through **Kosmas**. At the heart of the village is a huge platia shaded by the inevitable Platanos trees and a restaurant to tempt the weary traveller. Beyond the village on the right lies a picnic area and viewpoint for those with their own food. From here its all down hill for a time , at least until **Geraki** is reached. The road does not enter the town but crosses a major road leading into it. Geraki is a fairly large town which does not normally attract visitors even though there are the remains of an acropolis to view with cyclopean walls dating back to Mycenaean times. Anyone wishing to explore medieval Geraki, which lies a few kilometres south-east of the town, should enquire in the village for directions. There are the remains of some fifteen medieval churches and a castle to explore.

Olive groves dominate the scenery again as the fertile plain is crossed to **Vrontamas** (Vrondamas) a large, sprawling farming community. Rolling hills and wooded valleys add a new texture to the landscape especially around Grammousa, another sprawling village. Turn left for Monemvasia (signposted 50km/31 miles) as the main road is reached and expect a little more traffic for the final leg of the journey. The road leads directly to the causeway and the bridge to Monemvasia. It is possible to drive a little further around the south side of the rock but vehicles cannot enter the old town and there is not too much parking space. The modern village of Gefira has sprung up to the west of the causeway with hotels, tavernas and all necessary facilities to cater for the passing tourist trade.

Monemvasia has made its own mark on history if only for its Malmsey wine which was well known throughout Europe in the Middle Ages. Do not look too hard for the vineyards because the wine was imported from Crete and the Aegean islands which tells something of its importance as a trading post in those times.

Situated on the southern side of a rocky promontory which is around 1½km (1 mile) long and 250m (820ft) high, it takes its name from the fact that there is only one entrance (*mone embasis*). Its significant history dates from the Middle Ages, from the time when the local Greeks took refuge there and fortified it against the invading Slavs. Its development into a sound fortress and important trading post made it a target for invaders. In 1147 it managed to repulse an attack from the Normans of Sicily but faired less well against William de Villehardouin, fourth in succession of the princes of Achaea, in 1249, although the siege had lasted 3 years. It was the same William who founded Mistra. After a mere 15 years, amidst the complexities of medieval history, William was forced to cede this fortress, and Mistra, to Michael Palaiologos as ransom payment. In this period of Byzantine rule, it became the seat of the governor of the Peloponnese, an important ecclesiastical centre and a flourishing port with special trading concessions. Its chequered history was not quite finished for in 1460 it came into the hands of the Pope and in 1464 the Venetians. For a time it became a major centre of their Levantine trade in the east but its prosperity declined in the sixteenth century when it passed into Turkish control.

Once through the impressive arched entrance to the old town, the view is of narrow cobbled streets crowded by buildings in warm stone. Continuing ahead leads past souvenir shops and cafés to the small main square. It is very difficult to get an overview of the town but there are vantage points from the castle above or the sea shore below. It is worth the climb to the castle, not just for the view, but to amble around the extensive remains and to look around the restored church of Ag Sophia perched on the cliff end. In the main town few of the original forty churches remain and the most important of these is the cathedral dedicated to Christ in Chains (Elkomenos Christos), the largest medieval church in Laconia.

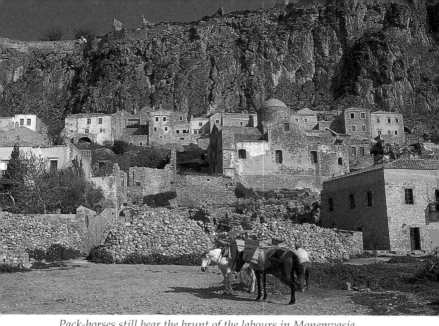

Pack-horses still bear the brunt of the labours in Monemvasia

The roof tops of Monemvasia, viewed from the castle above the town

Tour 2 • On To Deep Mani (185km/115 miles)

Mistra is easily worth half a day and there are some remains of ancient Sparta to inspect so the best option is to allow for an overnight stop in Mistra or nearby Sparti. Presently the one and only hotel in Mistra is the B class Byzantion (see Additional Information). There are a few rooms available around the village and a new hotel under construction. The first leg of the journey to Mistra is just over 100km (62 miles).

It is a question of backtracking first from Monemvasia to Skala, passing the road to Geraki. As the road climbs towards Krokeii (Krokee) views of the Taygetos range open up and particularly towards the peak Profitis Ilias which remains snow capped well into early summer. At the junction just beyond Krokeii turn right for Sparti (24km/15 miles). The red terra rosa earth paints the rolling landscape like a colour wash from an artists palette. Red soil gives way to yellow soil and to the left the Taygetos mountains rise abruptly from the Eurotas valley. Watered by streams from the Taygetos, this fertile plain produces endless crops between the groves of oranges and olives. Maize, wheat, barley and vegetables chase each other in endless succession.

The Sanctuary of Apollo at **Amekli** (Amykles), just 8km (5 miles) before Sparti, makes an interesting diversion. There is little now to see at the sanctuary but it does make a pleasant picnic spot situated on a hillock with magnificent views over the plains and mountains. Turn off right at Amekli and follow the signs. Do not worry when the road surface runs out since the location is only $1\frac{1}{2}$ km (1 mile) from the road.

Steadily increasing tractor traffic announces Sparti. Continue ahead to the centre and turn left for Mistra following the signs. Mistra lies 6km (4 miles) outside the town.

The new village of **Mistra**, situated around a road junction, is quite small. Unchanged by tourism, perhaps because it has little accommodation, the atmosphere is of an old Greek village with some really interesting tavernas run by the old folk. They are worth trying if only for the local rosé wine. The site of medieval Mistra (lower gate) lies 2km (1 mile) to the right as you enter the village. The site occupies a hillside position and has a top entrance, served by an outer road, in addition to the lower one.

Modern Sparti, the capital of Laconia, is a busy agricultural centre. Built as recently as 1834 on the site of the ancient city, it has a grid structure of straight streets lined with orange trees. There is little to entice the present tourist except that it has a number of hotels convenient for Mistra and, of course, the museum. Tucked away to the north of the city are some remains of ancient Sparti which are worth seeking out if only to enjoy the solitude of the location and the superb views of the Taygetos. To find it head for the stadium and keep going around and beyond onto a narrow cobbled road which rises up onto a wooded knoll with space to park.

Ancient Sparti was formed as early as 1000BC when invading Dorians subjugated a number of villages. Their place in history is assured by the harsh regimes practised and their military approach to life. Strict rules governed all aspects of life and determined the physical training both men and women should endure. Boys from the age of 7, provided that they had survived earlier tests of endurance, were trained under harsh supervision. Tough living conditions, deliberately inadequate food and physical endurance tests were all part of the course. The accent was strongly on the physical with total disregard to intellectual development. To add to their mystique, doors were closed to outsiders. Gradually the Spartans exerted their power over the whole of the Peloponnese except Argos. Whenever wars were around the Spartans had a role; the Persian Wars, the Messenian War and the Peloponnesian War (431-404BC). A succession of defeats followed which saw the gradual decline of the Spartans as a power until they were forced to join the Achaian League in 221BC.

Their physical approach to life left no room for pursuing the arts or fine architecture which characterised other civilisations throughout Greece. It seems contradictory that Homer should depict Helen, the most beautiful woman in the world, as a Spartan, a race that eschewed art, grace and beauty. Helen, wife of Agamemnon's younger brother Menelaus, was abducted by Paris son of King Priam of Troy. According to Homer's *The Iliad*, this was the cause of the Trojan War.

Thucydides, an Athenian historian, said of Sparta that if the town were laid waste and there remained only temples and foundations of their buildings, it would be hard to believe that the power of the town corresponded to its fame. Now you can see for yourself.

The site is open with free access. Nothing is marked which makes it difficult to identify many of the locations with certainty. The theatre, south-west side of the Acropolis hill, is the most obvious. It has been excavated to some extent and a few rows of seats are exposed. Acropolis hill itself is distinguished by the remains of two Byzantine churches. To the south lies the Agora well sprinkled with olive trees and still to the south are the remains of a building which is believed to be a Sanctuary to Leonidas.

Mistra (Mystras) lies on the east face of one of the foothills of the Taygetos. The lower entrance gate lies at an altitude of around 350m (1,148ft) while the castle on the summit tops 600m (1968ft). Footpaths weave all over. In practical terms it means there is a lot of walking and climbing involved; wear sensible shoes and allow plenty of time. An alternative for those not comfortable with uphill walking is to taxi to the upper entrance by the castle and wander down through the site. The walk described in the feature box starts at the top entrance and provides a quite spectacular return route for those who enjoy countryside walking.

Unlike other ancient sites in Greece and probably because of its size, Mistra is not subject to an annual treatment with weedkiller. Goats too are excluded. The consequence is that the site provides an exhibition of wild flowers throughout the spring months, including wild orchids, and all can be seen from the footpaths. Some of the species spotted in early April include the tall purple perennial honesty (*Lunaria rediviva*), the beautiful red anemone (*A. pavonina*), the ubiquitous yellow *Alyssum saxatile* growing on every rock, the delicate white flowered *Saxifraga chrysosplenifolia*, the dark blue *Muscari commutatum*, purple toadflaxa (*Cymbalaria microcalyx*) and at least three orchids; the yellow bee orchid (*Ophrys lutea*), the somewhat rarer bee orchid (*Ophrys spruneri*) and the giant orchid (*Barlia robertiana*). The list could be extended to include *Onosma frutescens* which droops its reddish yellow bells from rock crevice, yellow Euphorbias, tall spiky Asphodels, yellow and white daises in abundance and perhaps the greatest glory of all, the purple Judas tree, *Cercis siliquastrum* , but it still only represents a fraction of the species present.

Mistra did not emerge through the mists of time, it crystallised in 1249. William II de Villehardouin decided to build a castle on the hill, known then as Mesythra, in order to protect the fertile Eurotas valley. Under this Frankish influence, the name soon corrupted to Mistra. A few years later William was captured by Michael Palaiologos and, in 1262, after 3 years imprisonment, he was forced to cede his three fortresses, Mistra, Monemvasia and Maina (in the Mani), to Byzantium to gain his freedom. Mistra became the centre of resistance for the next 50 years until the Greeks had recovered most of the Morea, as the Peloponnese was then called. The seat of government moved from Monemvasia to Mistra and, ruled by despots, descendants of the emperor, it enjoyed a long period of prosperity. It attracted intellectuals, scholars, theologians and artists who thrived in the blossoming Byzantine culture. The Ottoman Turks brought the beginning of the end when they captured the city

A Mistra Circuit On Foot

There is a spectacular countryside return route from the top gate at Mistra which emerges eventually on the road between the village and the bottom gate. It requires about 45 minutes on foot and is only recommended for experienced walkers since navigation skills are required from the point where an obvious track finishes and another path is located. Sensible shoes are an absolute necessity.

Ignore the road to the right on leaving the top gate at Mistra and turn left instead. Pass beneath the archway and bear right a little to join a wide track which starts into immediate descent. Goat bells, snow capped peaks on the towering mountains and flower filled meadows instantly bring an alpine feel to the walk. After around 10 minutes walking the track ends at gates into a small holding and this is where some self-naviga-

The magnificent view from the summit of Mistra

tion is required. The tactic is to work around the fenced enclosure to pick up a path on the far side, a slightly longer diversion than first imagined. From just before the gates take a small path right, heading back uphill, broadly following the perimeter of the

Wild flowers such as Cyclamen repandum *can be found*

fence on the left. The path gradually leads around to the left and down into a wooded depression; find the way left, downhill through the woods, to join a distinct path almost immediately. Turn left downhill with a valley to the right. Continue ahead as the path runs into another and becomes stronger.

Many of the wild flowers are the same as those seen in Mistra but there are more besides like the blue iris (*I. unguicularis*), the delicate anemone so popular in gardens (*A. blanda*) and, towards the end of the walk, two small colonies of *Cyclamen repandum.*

A goat pen on the left is passed after about 20 minutes

and from here it is possible to see Sparti in the distance. The well trodden path winds down the valley to a small river which is crossed easily on available stones. Once over, turn left to take the lesser of two paths (the other goes ahead and up) and it is a scramble over rocks for a few minutes until a beautiful old cobbled trail is joined. Follow this into narrow jaws as the gorge closes around only to emerge with startling suddenness onto the plain and back into Mistra. At the outskirts of the village, fork left towards the church to arrive at the top of the one-way system between the site and the village. Left returns in 20 minutes to the lower gate and right to the village.

Mistra

in 1460. It remained prosperous on silk trade for a time and thrived again for a spell under Venetian rule (1687-1715) but it rapidly declined when the Turks returned. It was destroyed by the Albanians in 1790 and was abandoned completely when Sparti was rebuilt in 1834.

Apart from the beauty of the site and the pleasure of rambling its many footpaths, the numerous Byzantine churches and the Frankish castle on the summit are the main points of interest. The Monemvasia gate divides the upper town where the privileged classes lived apart from the lower town. The oldest churches are found in the lower town. The Mitropolis, the church of Dimitrios built in 1309, lies to the right from the lower entrance and adjoining is a small museum. Further along lies the monastic complex of Vrontochion which was the burial place of the despots. The only occupied building is the Pantanassa Convent, part way up the hill, but the nuns welcome visitors and the opportunity to display their handicrafts. Through the Monemvasia gate, little can be seen of the Palace of the Despots since this is currently under restoration. The Frankish castle on the very summit is worth the climb if only for the magnificent views of the Taygetos. Although built by the Franks, the castle was significantly rebuilt by the Turks.

The onward route from Mistra to Areopolis (80km/50 miles) demands little in the way of navigational skills. The first part of the journey offers the opportunity to review the landscape from a different perspective as the outward route is retraced as far as Hania. Distant vistas shrink as the road winds through the foothills of the Taygetos. New road sections cut many twists and turns off the old route and hasten the arrival at Githion.

Githion (Gythion), the port of both ancient and modern Sparti, is an attractive base for exploring the Mani. Neo-classical houses built in tiers up the hillside look over a summer trade of tour boats disgorging passengers for Mistra. Offshore is the islet of Marathonisi now connected to the mainland by a causeway. For the romantics, Marathonisi is believed to be the ancient Kranai where Paris took refuge with Helen on his way back to Troy.

Beyond Githion, the countryside remains pastoral with valleys filled with broad-leaved trees and there is no hint yet of Mani terrain. It changes once the turn off to Vlahos is passed. Suddenly the countryside takes on a barren look where even the olive trees crouch against the wind. A filling station greets your arrival at Areopolis where the town lies off the main road to the right.

Tour 3 • Deep Mani (110km/68 miles)

This route around the Mani is a pleasure to drive, surfaces are mostly good but care is needed in the most southerly section beyond Vathia. Care is needed too through the villages where the road often narrows appreciably. The circuit described traces the scenic east coast first to catch the morning sunlight lighting up the hillsides. Reaching the caves before they close at 3pm can be a problem for early season visitors and they may opt to reverse the route. It is no problem in high season when the caves remain open until 7pm. Do not expect too much from the villages, Areopolis is the largest and the others considerably smaller but are worth visiting for their tower houses, delightful location or old-world atmosphere. Some are fairly basic but others may have a shop or taverna.

The Mani is for the curious, for those fascinated by a peep into a private and very unruly past. There is beauty enough in the barren, treeless hills and rocky coastline but as an environment to prosper in it offers no encouragement. Every scrap of land brought into cultivation has to be fought for against the unyielding, rocky and stony terrain. Terracing clings impossibly to mountain faces defying nature in a search for crop space. Even the olive trees in the stony meadows are small and wind cut. Geographically isolated and with such a harsh environment it is a place to seek refuge rather than a place to settle. Wherever the refugees arrived from, and certainly some were from Sparta, they proved to be as hard and tough as their surroundings. Hostile to outside interference, they managed to remain independent from the Venetians, Franks and Turks. Their isolation went deeper. The villages too lived in isolation and were ruled by local chieftains in an atmosphere of constant friction and warring between the clans. The Maniots were notorious too for feuding between themselves and indulged in vendettas which were long and bitter, protracted over generations. Square built tower houses rising to several stories were built for safety, many of which still stand grouped on the hillsides. Their fighting qualities were respected in the War of Independence in 1821 when many of their generals distinguished themselves but the pressure for the Mani to join the new state following the end of the war was not welcomed. One consequence of the continuing dispute was the assassination by a Maniot of John Kapodistras, the first elected leader of the new independent Greece. Eventually, in 1834, Mani reluctantly agreed to join the independent state.

Feuding is now a thing of the past and visitors are welcomed by the Maniots with a full measure of the usual Greek hospitality. A local

The shingle beach and shore line at Kokkala

One of the many tiny tower house hamlets on the way to the southern tip of the Mani peninsula

A typical Greek house in the village of Flemohori

Flowers Of The Mani

In spite of the barren and hostile appearance of the landscape for much of the year, spring time is very colourful. The hillsides support pink and white cistus bushes and masses of spiny brooms, spanish broom and euphorbias all which splash yellow about very freely. Against this background the occasional purple Judas trees in bloom really shines out. Cultivated ground swarms with white daisies, yellow crucifers, pink geraniums, purple echiums and wild gladioli. Amongst these are a surprising number of wild

Orchis papilionacea
(pink butterfly orchid)

orchids like the pink butterfly (*Orchis papilionacea*), the purple *Orchis mascula* and the pink pyramidal orchid (*Anacamptis pyramidalis*). The bee orchids might be harder to spot but they are present in numbers including the yellow bee (*Ophrys lutea*), the saw-fly orchid (*O. tenthredinifera*) and *O. spruneri*. One other fascinating orchid is the pink-flowered *Orchis Italica*, the naked man orchid, in which the individual flowers are man-shaped. It takes its common name from the small appendage between the 'legs.'

From Areopolis To Ag Sotiras On Foot

This is only a short walk taking 30 to 40 minutes in total. Ag Sotiras, or Kouscouri as it was once called, is a partly deserted village lying just east of Areopolis.

Set off from the large square in Areopolis to cross the main road and enter a narrow road opposite. Already Ag Sotiras can be seen on the hillside ahead. As the surfaced road swings away left, keep ahead to join a cobbled trail which becomes stepped just below the village. The lower village is mostly deserted but there are more signs of life in the upper part. The large open area in front of the church provides fine elevated views of the surrounding area. Return to Areopolis the same way.

comment suggested that the young men have not lost their aggression but now channel it into serving in the armed forces. Many of the tower houses are still around and some are being converted by the EOT (Greek National Tourist Office) for tourist accommodation.

Areopolis is the capital of the Mani. Its spacious platia, which serves as a bus terminus and where the best tavernas are located, seems like something of an after thought. It is appended to a tangle of narrow streets crowded with grey stone houses. In the midst of these lies the church of the Taxiarchis built in 1798 which shows a Byzantine eagle above the main door. One of the EOT guest houses nearby has a private museum of Maniot weapons, small canons, daggers, swords and rifles, which are displayed in a window for outside viewing. The Saturday market adds colour to the town. On a practical note, Areopolis has the only bank in the region and this is part time, opening Tuesday and Thursday mornings only.

Leave Areopolis heading south but shortly watch for the left turn signposted Kotronas and Kokkala. The road climbs over the spine of the Mani. Slender cypress trees, like exclamation marks slashed on the landscape, are even more noticeable in this environment. The left turn down to Kotronas starts a short scenic run which offers beautiful coastal views. **Kotronas** itself is a mixture of sombre grey towers and bright white houses. It has a taverna and a shop. Retrace the route back to the main road and continue south. The very next village, **Flemohori**, is worth a stop to see the exceptionally tall tower house there. Further south, the cluster of tower houses sprawling down the hillside is the village of Paxanika. That too has some tall towers. **Kokkala**, the next stop en route, is a picturesque village on the sea front with a bakery and tavernas. The broad sweep of shingle beach leads the eye to a church located right on the shore line.

Small villages slip by with southerly progress, most with tower houses and some totally deserted. After the tower house village of Lagia, the road takes a new course across the tail of the peninsula to meet the western coast road. Turn left here for **Vathia**. The small, tight cluster of tower houses perched on a hillock overlooking the sea is Vathia. It is worth a stop to wander around amidst these buildings which are in various stages of restoration to tourist accommodation. The final section of the southern journey re-crosses the peninsula to the east coast village of **Porto Kagio**, the end of the road. This tiny port with its modern cube style houses is located on a beautiful bay and boasts what is probably the most southerly taverna in mainland Greece. It is possible to walk further south to the very tip of the peninsula.

Retrace the route through Vathia to start the west coast leg of the tour. **Gerolimin** is hard to miss at the moment, the road plunges you into its very narrow streets. There is a wide by-pass road not far from completion so it may soon be necessary to turn off to visit. Set in a barren wilderness, it is another village of mixed old tower houses and modern cubes around a shingle bay but not without character. Not only does it boast a taverna and a post office but it also has a hotel and rooms. A narrow coastal plain ribbons along the west coast keeping the road off the mountain side and some of the visual impact is lost. The tiny fishing village of **Mezapos** lies just over 2km (1 mile) from the main road but the route down to it is on a concrete track just wide enough for one car. It is famed locally for its deep water harbour and its fish taverna.

Next stop is the spectacular **Diros Caverns** (Pyrgos Dirou), just 7km (4 miles) short of Areopolis. These caves are very much on the tourist route so expect queues in summer. The trip round the caves, which takes around 25 minutes, takes place in small boats which glide noiselessly through 1km ($1\frac{1}{2}$ mile) of illuminated passages and caverns. It is an entirely visual experience with no commentary on the various rock formations. Head room is tight in some passages. There are occasions, and the wind is a factor, when the water levels are too low for the caves to open.

Additional Information

Places to Visit

Mistra
Open: daily 8.30am-3pm but the museum inside is closed on Monday.

Sparti
Museum
Open: 8.30am-3pm. Closed on Monday.

Accommodation

HOTELS
* = Open all year

Areopolis: TELEPHONE PREFIX 0733
*Hotel Mani** (C)
12 Agiou Petrou Square
☎ 51269/51397

Pension Londas (A) ☎ 51360
*Pension Pyrgos Kapetanakou** (A)
☎ 51233

Pension Tsimoba (Traditional House)
☎ 51301

GITHION: TELEPHONE PREFIX 0733
*Hotel Githion** (A)
☎ 23523/23452/23777

Hotel Belle Helene (B)
Vathi Ageranou
☎ 22867/9

*Hotel Laryssion** (C)
71 I. Grigoraki
☎ 22021/6

*Hotel Milton** (C)
Mavrovouni
☎ 22091/22914/5

*Hotel Pantheon**(C)
33 Vas Pavlou
☎ 22284/89

MISTRA: TELEPHONE PREFIX 0731
Hotel Byzantion (B but expect E standard), Vas Sophias ☎ 93309
Best accommodation is in nearby Sparti.

MONEMVASIA: TELEPHONE PREFIX 0732
*Hotel Minoa** (C)
14 Spartis
☎ 61209/61224

*Pension Ano Malvasia** (A)
☎ 61323/61113

*Pension Malvasia II** (A) ☎ 61323
Pension Castro (A) ☎ 61413/4
*Pension Malvasia** (B) ☎ 61323/61435
*Pension Monemvassia** (B) ☎ 62381
Furnished Apartments Panos (B)
☎ 61480

SPARTI: TELEPHONE PREFIX 0731
*Hotel Lida**(B)
☎ 23601/2

*Hotel Menelaion**(B)
91 K. Paleologou
☎ 22161/5

*Hotel Apollo**(C)
14 Thermopilon
☎ 22491/3

*Hotel Dioscouri**(C)
94 Likourgou & Atreidon
☎ 28484/28666

*Hotel Laconia**(C)
61 K. Paleologou
☎ 28951/2

*Hotel Maniatis**(C)
72 K. Paleologou
☎ 22665/9

*Hotel Sparti Inn**(C)
105 Thermopilon
☎ 21021/6 & 22021

Traditional Settlements run by the EOT
Kastro Monemvasias:
Xenonas Kellia (12 rooms)
☎ 0732 61520

Vathia (Mani): Telephone prefix 0733

Pirgos Exarhakou (4 rooms) ☎ 54229
Pirgos Giannoakakou (2 rooms) ☎ 54229
Pirgos Keramida (3 rooms) ☎ 54229
Pirgos Mitsakou (3 rooms) ☎ 54229
Pirgos Papadongona ☎ 54229
Pirgos Tselepi ☎ 54229

Camping

* = Open all year

Agadeika
Gythion Beach Hellenic Camping
☎ 0733 23441

Gythion
Meltemi
☎ 0733 22833/23260

Mavrovouni
Mani Beach
☎ 0733 23450/1, 01 8931810

Mistra
Castle View
☎ 0731 93384, 01 3212812

Monemvasia
Capsis
☎ 0732 611123

Neochori
Porto Ageranos
☎ 0733 22039

Skala Glykovryssis
Lykourgos
☎ 0735 91580/2, 01 3611496

Slaviki, Mistra
*Mistras**
☎ 0731 22724

Vathi
Kronos
☎ 0733 24124, 01 6468453

Transport

Public Transport

By Bus: Around 7 buses a day run between Athens and Sparti, a journey of around 4½ hours. From Sparti buses run to Mistra, Monemvasia and Areopolis. One bus daily travels Athens-Monemvasia (7 hours). Gythion, for Mani, is served by four buses daily from Athens (5½ hours) Within Mani, local buses are limited to two per day down the west coast and one down the east. By Boat: there is a summer hydrofoil service Piraeus/Monevasia from Zea Marina in Piraeus.

4

THE WESTERN PELOPONNESE

This tour, which completes the circuit of the Peloponnese, visits the remaining four provinces. First is Messinia, the garden of Greece, a region tucked away in the south-west corner which attracts perhaps fewer visitors than other provinces. The reasons can only be geographical but with an ever improving road system it must be set to change for it has much to interest the traveller. It is another *nome* which has a strong vein of historical interest from the ancient through to medieval. Homer addicts revel in Nestor's Palace where one archaeological find was a bathtub which has been brilliantly restored and placed in its original location. *The Odyssey* relates how Telemachus, son of Odysseus, visits King Nestor seeking news of his father. Whilst there, the beautiful Polycaste, youngest daughter of the king, gives Telemachus a bath and rubs him with olive oil so he emerges looking like a king. Like many other visitors, you can stand, look at the bathtub and wonder! The whole site is evocative but so too is the site of ancient Messini (Ithomi) situated some 24km (15 miles) north of the modern capital. It is a natural stronghold and a splendid setting for an ancient site. Down on the Messinian peninsula are two fine examples of medieval fortifications, the twin citadels of Methoni and Koroni both of which are visited in Tour 2 from Pylos. Pylos, standing at the southern end of Navarino Bay, is the most attractive resort in the region and a convenient base for exploration. Kalamata, the largest city of the southern Peloponnese suffered a massive earthquake in 1986 which killed twenty people and destroyed thousands of homes. Today it has largely recovered from that disaster but it remains a bustling industrial and market town which has a Frankish castle, a museum and some Byzantine churches to explore but the motorist can expect to tangle with congested traffic and find difficulty in parking.

The remaining three provinces are less extensively explored, particularly Arkadia which is entered only to visit the mountain village of Karitena to admire the castle and the old bridge featured on the 5,000 *drachma* note. Ilia, the *nome* immediately north of Messinia, has a site of antiquity known throughout the world; Olympia, home of the Olympic games. Like Delphi, it is one of Greece's major tourist attractions but, in spite of that, the commercialisation is still relatively low key. Heading north-east from Olympia, the final leg of the Peloponnese tour cuts through the province of Achaia to visit Kalavrita and the famous rack and pinion railway which descends from there through the spectacular Vouraikos Gorge to Diakopto.

Tour 1 • Outer Mani (140km/87 miles)

Improvements to sections of the coastal road from Areopolis to Kalamata are in progress. There may be dusty stretches to face in these parts but otherwise the road is asphalted and generally good. Taken leisurely, and both the winding nature of the road and the dramatic scenery demand that it is taken leisurely, the full journey takes around 5 hours. Stoupa and Messini offer alternative stopping points if time is short.

Heading north from Areopolis, the coast road signposted Kalamata is soon reached. Scenic interest starts almost immediately as the road by-passes **Limini** which lies by the sea shore in an attractive bay. At the north end of the bay is Karavostasi, a tiny port serving **Itylo**, a village teeming with tower houses which has the distinction of being a former capital of the Mani. Sandwiched between the slopes of the Taygetos mountains and the sea, northerly progress along the route is punctuated with cameo views around every bend. Wandering coastlines, tower houses, olive groves, grazing sheep, slender cypress trees, steep mountain slopes, Byzantine churches and tiny villages chase each other in endless procession. Good beaches run north from above the small fishing village of Ag Nikolaos. **Stoupa**, with its delightful bays, has the best of the beaches, undoubtedly the best in the Mani region. Tourist developments are slowly turning Stoupa into a resort area but for the moment it remains an acceptable blend of new whitewashed villas and old mellow houses with pensions and tavernas. **Kardamili**, further north, claims to be the top resort and it certainly has more sophistication if that is measured in tourist shops and fast food places. Its small harbour looks onto a fortified offshore island. The beach there is pebbly but good for swimmers.

OLYMPIA
🏛 Archaeological Museum
🏛 Museum of Olympic Games

Platanos
Olympia
Makrisia
Krestena
Grillos
Kalithea
Platiana
Andritsena
ILIA
Temple Of Apollo
Epikourios
Bassae
Karitena
Megalopoli
ARCADIA
Zevgolatio
Meligalas
Neohorion
Ancient Messini
(Ithomi)
Mavromati
MESSINIA
Arsinoi
Lambena
LACONIA
Eva
Triodos
MESSINIA
Metamorphosis
Messini
Kalamata
Vlachopoulo
Nestor's Palace
Hora
Rizomilo
Sotirianika
Kazarma
Stavropigio
Petalidi
Kardamili
Neokastro
Stoupa
Pylos
Ag Andreas
Ag Nikolaos
Platsa
Methoni
Lamia
Nomitsi
Finikounda
Koroni

**THE WESTERN
PELOPONNESE**
STOUPA TO OLYMPIA

0   30km

0   20 miles

While the character of the Mani may wain with progress beyond
Kardamili, this is not true of the scenery. The road winds into the tree
clad mountains and is breathtakingly scenic near Stavropigio where
the road plunges to cross a gorge and climbs away back into the hills.
Traffic density increases as Kalamata nears but the main road by-
passes the town centre and flirts only with the outskirts. **Messini** is
adequately signed and fairly soon reached. Again the main road is

A small Byzantine church within the fortress at Koroni

Messinia, The Garden Of Greece

The extraordinary luxuriance and fertility of the region has been recognised since ancient times and it is not without justification that Messinia has been labelled Graecia Felix, the Garden of Greece. Somehow the geography and climate have conspired to produce growing conditions found nowhere else in the country. Mountains shelter the plains from the cold northern winds and provide the water for irrigation while the southern sun and warm winds from Africa turn it into a hothouse. Currant vines are an important commercial crop and one product for which the region is locally famous is its currant brandy. Kalamata too claims to grow the tastiest olives in the whole of Greece and Kalamata olive oil is recognised as the finest available. It is without a doubt the best buy to take home but look for virgin oil which is obtained from the first pressings. This is the very highest quality, superb for salad dressing and usually available in 5 litre sealed tins.

Everything grows well but figs are another fruit which are economically important. Petalidi, visited in Tour 2, claims to grow the best in Greece. The list is extensive but the other product worthy of mention is the mulberry tree. From the time the Chinese silk worm was brought to Europe, the mulberry proliferated and it grew especially well in Messinia. The silk trade it produced passed through the port of Methoni in medieval times. First the Turks destroyed the trees during the War of Independence and then disease decimated the silk worm to all but destroy the industry. In spite of these difficulties, the silk trade still survives and silk handkerchiefs and scarves are a speciality of the region.

kept away from the town centre and once beyond it is back into pastoral countryside. Olive groves, vineyards and white farm houses hide amongst the low rolling hills. There are tantalising glimpses of the harbour on the descent into Pylos where the main road leads down to the waterfront. There is some parking around the platia by the harbour and more on the road which continues past the harbour along the sea front.

Pylos, earlier known as Navarino, sits looking out into Navarino Bay. It is a small town with some elegance and style with its arcaded streets and large shady platia. It has its own place in history on account of the famous naval battle which took place in the bay on 20 October 1827 and which proved to be a turning point in Greece's struggle for independence from Turkish rule. In the Treaty of London 1827, it was agreed that Britain, France and Russia should guarantee the autonomy of Greece and send a joint fleet to enforce an armistice on the warring parties. In spite of orders not to engage in battle, the fleet sailed into the bay as a show of force when the Turks had refused an armistice. Shots fired by an Egyptian ship on the Turkish side started a fierce battle in which 26 men-of-war of the allies faced up to 82 warships of the Turko-Egyptian fleet. Within the space of a few hours the Turkish fleet lost 63 ships and was almost annihilated without the loss of a single allied vessel.

From the time the French troops arrived under the command of General Maison to rebuild the town, it slowly abandoned its name of Navarino in favour of Pylos but it should not be confused with the classical site of Pylos, the home of King Nestor, which lies some 17km (10 miles) away at the north end of the bay.

Just south of the town, 10 minutes on foot from the harbour, is the Turko-Venetian fortress of **Neokastro** which was rebuilt by the French in 1829 and later used as a prison. The extensive boundary walls enclose a defended area wherein lies a church converted from a domed mosque. Some landscaping is in progress which includes a picnic area and, whilst opening hours are observed, access to the fortress is free.

Tour 2 • The Peninsula Tour (150km/93 miles)

With the twin medieval castles of Methoni and Koroni to visit and Nestor's Palace, this tour happily fills out a day. If there is a problem with the timing, it is the restriction imposed by the mid-afternoon closing times of the sites visited en route. At least they all have early opening hours. The unclassified roads used to cross the southern end of the peninsula, between Methoni and Koroni, were all well surfaced and presented only the usual pothole hazard.

Leaving Pylos on the Messini road, take the left turn, signposted Pyrgos, less than 3km (2 miles) outside the town. Nestor's Palace is only signposted as it is reached, just before the village of Hora.

Nestor's Palace is beautifully situated on a hill overlooking Navarino Bay. First explored in 1939 by Carl Blegen, World War II intervened and it was only fully excavated in 1952. Little stands above foundation height but the complex ground plan is clearly defined and the rooms are all labelled with good on site information. The museum housing many of the artefacts is in the nearby village of Hora.

The impressive fortress at Methoni

Although the site was occupied from around 2000BC, the royal palace was not developed until Mycenaean times, around 1300BC. Two storied buildings were built with the extensive use of wood in columns, half timbered walls, roofs and ceilings. Its final destruction was by fire around 1200BC and, with so much wood involved, little remains of the upper story apart from objects.

King Nestor, son of Neleus, was a contemporary of Agamemnon of Mycenae. His kingdom was rich, flourishing on the agricultural wealth of the region. He fought alongside Agamemnon in the protracted Trojan Wars when, in the 'catalogue of ships' he was credited with supplying ninety vessels, second in numbers only to Agamemnon. Nestor features strongly in Homer's *The Iliad* and *The Odyssey* depicted as a wise elder statesman whom Agamemnon valued as a trusted councillor. It was to Nestor that Telemachus turned for guidance when his father, Odysseus, failed to return from the Trojan Wars.

Apart from the rich Homeric associations, there is another story to relate which is romantic in a different sense. In the search for the site of Nestor's Palace and encouraged by the number of tholos tombs around, Blegen chose to start excavations on the hill known as Epano Englianos. Hundreds of inscribed clay tablets were unearthed

The azure blue sea at Finikounda

within hours on the very first day of digging. Unfortunately on that same day, following Italy's invasion of Albania, Greece was drawn into World War II and the tablets were removed to Athens for storage in a bank vault until after the war. It was not until 1952 that work was able to start again when more of the tablets were found. Experts agreed that these were different from the Linear A script used by the Minoans and were designated Linear B but Blegen and other scholars like Sir Arthur Evans were convinced that the language was Minoan. The break through in translating this script came not from an historian or archaeologist but from an architect, Michael Ventris. He believed Linear B to be an archaic form of Greek and progressed by assigning values to the frequently recurring signs until a breakthrough was achieved with the word 'tripod.'

From Nestor's Palace continue ahead towards the village of **Hora** and pick up signs for the museum. This is located by the junction with the Kalamata road. The museum adds significantly to a visit to the palace and shows some of the Linear B clay tablets found there as well as frescos and pottery.

Take the Kalamata road from Hora through Metamorphosis and Vlachopoulo to rejoin the Pylos/Messini road. Still heading towards Messini and Kalamata, look, as the road narrows to pass through the village of Rizomilo, for the right turn to Koroni. This route meets up with the coast at **Petalidi**, a large village with an attractive platia situated in the grand sweep of a sandy bay. Yellow blossom of broom and the purple of the Judas trees light the way along the fast coastal road down to Koroni.

The fortified village of **Koroni** with its narrow, sometimes stepped streets, wrought iron balconies and white houses is one of those towns which is unmistakably Greek. The harbour front is lined with fish tavernas and all that is missing is a beach although there is one some 2km (1 mile) south of the town. From the parking area on the sea front, the castle is reached by walking inland a block then following the narrow stepped streets to the south. The fortress, built by the Byzantines, enlarged by the Franks and added to by the Turks is now largely walls. Although the ruins may not be as impressive as Methoni, its position on the headland looking towards Mani and the Taygetos is superb. The area inside the walls is given over to houses and gardens but there is also the nunnery of Timiou Prodromou and a small Byzantine church nearby.

Leave Koroni by the same route but watch out for a left turn on a bend just 5km (3 miles) from the harbour front. This is the road through **Finikounda** which cuts across the southern tip of the peninsula. It is a scenic run winding through the valleys giving a view of Lamia slumbering on a low hilltop. The approach to Finikounda provides a spectacular view just as the road starts a descent into it. It is a small picturesque resort enjoying a fine position looking onto a sandy bay. Blankets draped from balconies of the whitewashed houses suggest this is more of a residential village than a resort but it is popular with the Greeks in summer. Farmland cultivation dominates the scenery increasingly and an array of polythene greenhouses announces **Methoni**. The town is entered by a very narrow bridge.

The fortress at Methoni is as impressive as any in Greece. Its massive walls and bastions are lapped on three sides by the sea and isolated by a moat. Such is its domination that the modern town is swamped by it but the facilities offered to tourists by way of hotels and beaches do not go unnoticed.

Once called Pedasos, Methoni is known from antiquity and was referred to by Homer as 'rich in vines.' It was not until the Middle Ages that it became commercially important under Venetian control as did Koroni. Apart from trading in silk and vines, it was used as a port of call for pilgrims en route to the Holy Land. Whatever fortifications there might have been, they were strengthened by the Venetians and the walls on the west side defended by five towers are part of their construction. It fell to the Turks in 1500 and was recovered by the Venetians in 1686 but fell again to the Turks in 1715. It remained in Turkish hands until liberated by French troops under General Maison in 1826 following the battle of Navarino Bay. All these occupations have left an imprint on the construction of the fortress which throughout these times sheltered a sizeable town. The long narrow bridge leading to the Venetian arched entrance was rebuilt by the French in 1828 who actually pulled down the medieval town in the centre and rebuilt it in its present position on the mainland. The road north from Methoni leads fairly quickly to Pylos, a distance of some 12km (7 miles).

Tour 3 • North To Olympia (255km/158 miles)

This may not be the obvious way to Olympia but it is a scenically spectacular route taking in the ancient site of Messini and calling in at the mountain villages of Karitena and Andritsena along the way. Karitena offers a castle and a beautiful old bridge and Andritsena just good mountain ambience. Both villages offer accommodation for an overnight stop but expect to find only rooms in Karitena. The short diversion to see the remarkably well preserved temple at Bassae is from Andritsena. It is not a journey to be taken quickly,

The terracotta tiled roof top of the Byzantine church at Karitena

The Odeon at Ancient Messina, occupying a position of natural beauty

winding mountain roads restrict speed and there is too much to be savoured. An overnight stop at one of the two mountain villages is recommended.

Follow the road from Pylos as far as Messini and turn left off the by-pass road to enter the main square in the centre. Look for the sign to Meligalas and head north up this road, turning left at the unsigned T-junction shortly encountered. Olive groves and Judas trees predominate as small farming communities follow one after another. Turn left at Lambena to follow signs to Ithomi, which, incidentally, lies close to the village of Mavromati. The plains are left behind as the encroaching hills of Mount Ithomi draw ever nearer and a gentle ascent starts before the village of Arsinoi where old ladies in black dominate the population.

The hills get steeper as Mavromati is reached. The modern town is built part way up Mount Ithomi, above is the acropolis perched on the very crown of the hill and below, on the valley bottom, is the most important part of the ruins of **Ancient Messini (Ithomi)**. A signpost at the centre of the village indicates directions to the various parts of the ancient city. New roads are being cut down to the main site but access is by a steep, narrow concrete track which forks down to the left just about 100m (328ft) beyond the signpost. As with many of the ancient sites, it occupies a position of great natural beauty.

Protected by the 800m (2,624ft) high Mount Ithomi, Epameinondas chose this site in 371BC to build a stronghold to defend Messinia from the Spartans and allow the return of the Messinians to their country. This new fortified city formed a link with other strongholds stretching across Arcadia, including Megalopolis, Mantineia (Mandinia) and Argos, all ranged against Sparti. Diodorus claimed, somewhat extravagantly, the city was built in 85 days but considering that the circuit of walls alone was some 9km (6 miles) long, 4m (13ft) high and 2½m (8ft) thick, it would have been a mighty feat. The walls were strengthened by square or semicircular towers at intervals along its length.

On the valley bottom lies a square building thought to be an agora but possibly a Sanctuary of Asklepios. A small temple occupies the central position and to the outside is a colonnade. Nearby is a small theatre and to the west of the agora amongst the olive groves is a stadium. Much of the stone seating is roughly in position and the seating for the dignitaries has been reset. The main theatre, lying to the north of the stadium, is well overgrown and all that remains is the analemma wall.

Those with the time and energy to explore the acropolis can reach it by a path from the village or an alternative path via the Laconian

Horta

Outside the village of Arsinoi, one or two of the women were seen in the fields assiduously collecting leaves of a dandelion species to use as a vegetable. This is not especially a local habit, it can be seen all over Greece. Collectors are easily recognised, usually they have a knife in one hand and a polythene carrier bag bursting with green leaves in the other and eyes down searching the ground.

The leaves are first boiled in water, like cabbage and then well coated with oil and lemon and served as *horta*. It is often available in tavernas in season, which is throughout winter and spring, but not always on the menu. One reason is the translation problem and it is sometimes erroneously listed as spinach. Worth asking for if it is hot and freshly cooked but less appetising when cold and soaked too long in oil. High mountains produce the best *horta*.

Gate. On top of the mountain there is the abandoned sixteenth-century Monastery of Vourkano standing on the site of the Sanctuary of Zeus Ithomatas which is said to have witnessed human sacrifice. Myth claims that Zeus was born by a spring on the mountain and taken to the top by the nymphs Neda and Ithomi. Even today, Mavromati celebrates an annual festival which is believed to survive from the ancient feast to Zeus.

Leave Mavromati by continuing through the village to the Arcadian Gate from where fine stretches of the old city walls can be seen, particularly to the west. Turn right here to pass through the gate onto what may appear to be nothing more than a track but, fear not, the road is asphalted almost immediately beyond. It continues as a good road through some fine mountain scenery passing occasional small villages like Neohorion where the road may narrow and become rough as it often does through villages. **Meligalas** is a fairly large town with a road system which is not well signed. Turn right at the T-junction as the village is reached then left on meeting the major road in the centre to head out north, soon to run alongside the railway on the right. Once through the village of Zevgolatio, follow signs to Kalamata which means turning right at the complex road junction, before passing beneath the road bridge, to join the main road. Turn left at the next major junction following signs to Tripoli but only as far as **Megalopoli**, reached after a long wind up into the hills.

For Andritsena (44km/27 miles) follow around the platia in Megalopoli to the left. Just over 1km ($\frac{1}{2}$ mile) along this road there is the opportunity to detour left, just before the power station, to see the ancient theatre which has survived from around the fourth century BC when Megalopolis was founded as the capital of the federated states of Arcadia. Much of this ancient site has now disappeared and the theatre is all that remains of significance. Pausanias described it as the largest theatre in Greece built with seating for more than 20,000. Built against the north side of a hill, there is not so much to see now, only the front rows of seats are well preserved. The large power station nearby is rather dominant and adds nothing to the ambience.

Although the mountains are not far away, the road stays on the plain of Megalopolis for a time yet weaving its way through cultivated countryside. Shortly, where the castle on the pinnacle announces Karitena; stay ahead at the junction as the major road to Andritsena bends away to the left. Drive up into the village as far as possible and park in the large platia.

With stone built, red-roofed houses clustering around the base of a castle crowned hill, **Karitena** is nothing if not picturesque. A steep path to the castle is signposted out of the platia and it takes around 15 minutes on foot. At the fork part way up turn sharp right for the castle. Built by Hugh de Bruyeres in 1254, the walls are the best preserved part but there are the remains of a vaulted hall inside and a number of cisterns. The superb views alone make the climb worthwhile. Apart from the eleventh century church of Panagia, the other point of interest in Karitena is the old bridge which is featured on the 5,000 *drachma* note. The easiest way to see it is to stop on the main road as you drive along by it shortly after rejoining the Andritsena road but it is possible to walk footpaths down from the platia.

Leave Karitena by the same road and follow signs to **Andritsena**. To view the old bridge at close quarters, stop just after crossing the new bridge and find a small footpath down to the left. For a time scrub covered mountains dominate the scenery but distant vistas open up as the road winds up into the mountains and to Andritsena (765m/2,509ft). It is hard to tell now that it was once a major town throughout the years of Turkish occupation, except perhaps from the wooden houses which still remain. On a walk down the main street, crowded out with shops and houses with overhanging balconies, it is possible to see women weaving away making the woollen rugs which are sold locally. Andritsena is an attractive base from which to visit the temple at nearby Bassae but it is still not blessed with too many hotels. The superbly situated B class Xenia Hotel, just by the

A 5,000 Drachma Walk

The return walk from Karitena Castle takes around 1 hour and, while it is easy enough going down, remember the return is all uphill. The footpaths are stony too so that stout shoes or trainers are needed.

Leave the platia as for the castle but stay ahead immediately ignoring the castle route to the left. Follow the stony track which stays close to the castle hill on the left to emerge on a loop of the surfaced road. Leave the road straight away to continue downhill on a trail starting between two shrines which shortly crosses a track. Keep heading down until another track is reached then

The old bridge at Karitena is featured on the 5,000 drachma note

turn right to continue down in the direction of the new bridge; the old bridge lies alongside. About half of this medieval bridge remains in good order but the view through its arches back to the village, as shown on the 5,000 *drachma* note, is now masked by the new bridge.

Return by the same route as far as the two shrines on the surfaced road and now enter the track used on the downward leg. Almost immediately, take a narrow path off right to weave your way through the narrow village walkways back to the platia.

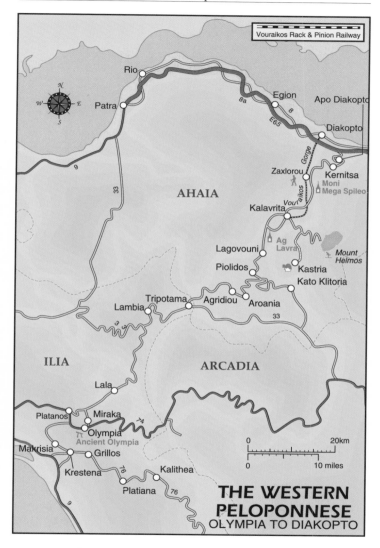

entrance to the village, is comfortable if somewhat austere although breakfast scored no points while the D class Hotel Pan in the centre of the village looks perhaps more homely.

Once through the crowded main street, turn left for the Temple of

Apollo Epikourios at **Bassae (Vassae)**. It is only a 14km (9 mile) drive but the route is scenically spectacular. The modern, asphalted road climbs up into the mountains and follows along ledges and skims in and around the peaks, always comfortably wide but with possible hazards from fallen rocks and edge subsidence.

Bassae means ravines which is an appropriate description for the site of this magnificent temple built on a terrace at an elevation of 1,131m (3,710ft) overlooking a deep ravine. The ancients built temples in locations appropriate to their dedication. A temple to Poseidon, like the one at Sounion in Attica, would be found near the sea and here, so close to the sun, it is no surprise to find the temple is dedicated to Apollo but this time he is attributed with another epithet, Epikourios (the saviour). Pausanias relates that it was built as a thanksgiving to Apollo for sparing them the plague which ravished much of the area during the Peloponnesian War. Constructed in the dark grey local marble, scholars still argue whether the temple was built before or after the Parthenon but generally agree on somewhere between 450 and 420BC.

Probably because nobody wanted the stone for other building purposes in this inhospitable part of the world, and because of its isolation, the temple has survived in a remarkable state of preservation. Its location was rediscovered by the Frenchman Jaochim Bocher in 1765 who was murdered by bandits on his return a year later. The British and Germans braved the lawlessness in 1811 and persuaded the Turks to sell pieces of the cella frieze which ended up in the British Museum. The temple now is protected by a huge tent, a remarkable structure in its own right, and it does add atmosphere once inside. It is the best preserved temple in Greece and most of the doric columns are still standing.

Return by the same route to Andritsena and from there follow the signs left to Kalithea (17km/10 miles) and Pyrgos. The appearance of pines brings a softness to the barren landscape as the road gradually descends out of the mountains. **Kalithea** with its wooden balconied, stone houses, some colourfully festooned in washing, is a village large enough for tavernas but without a bread shop. Olive trees appear after further descent and the hills give way to a rolling undulating landscape dotted with farms. **Krestena** is the biggest village en route with Hotel Athena and a restaurant but is no more than a ribbon development. Turn right through here following signs to Olympia and be prepared to weave through the narrow streets of the next village, Makrisia, before crossing the intensively cultivated plain to Olympia.

Olympia is a small modern village which has grown in response to the influx of tourism. Hotels and tourist shops dominate but, in spite of the commercialism, it is a pleasant enough place for a short stay to visit the site. It is perhaps busiest throughout the day when the coach trippers are allowed their regulated free time to wander but by evening everything quietens down very appreciably. Parking is permitted along one side of the road only and this alternates according to the month as indicated by the signs with either a single or a double vertical bar. For further information refer to the Travelling in Greece (Driving in Greece) section in the Fact File at the end of this guide.

It is famed throughout the world as the birthplace of the panhellenic Olympic games which took place here every 4 years from 776BC to AD393. Unlike other great cultural centres of the period, Olympia was never a great city. It was a sanctuary built in the middle of a fertile plain by a spring at the foot of Mount Kronos, around 2000BC, for the worship of Kronos, the father of Zeus, and the earth-goddess Rhea. The origin of the games is lost in a jumble of myths and legends. It may have started from a chariot race organised by King Oinomaos of Pisa who did not wish to lose his beautiful daughter Hippodameia by marriage. Suitors were invited to race their chariot against his to win his daughter but the penalty for losing was death. King Oinomaos was full of tricks to prevent being beaten but he was eventually outsmarted by Pelops. The linchpins in the King's chariot were replaced with some made of clay which held only long enough for the race to get underway. The King was killed in the accident and Pelops claimed his daughter. Alternatively, the origins may have been simpler. It is said that Heracles, son of the great Zeus who lived on Mount Olympos, marked out a sacred grove, the Altis, and introduced games in honour of his Olympian father.

In early Bronze Age religions, women and female deities were much in control and there is evidence to suggest that the early games involved women and remained that way until the worship of Zeus intruded. Myths and legends apart, the games were restarted in 776BC and the winners then and thereafter recorded. Pausanias claims that the prize first of all was for a footrace which was won in the first games by Koroibos of Elis. The race was over the distance of one stadion (192m/630ft). At the fourteenth Olympics, according to Pausanias, a two lap race was added and in the eighteenth the pentathlon (foot race, long jump, wrestling, javelin and discus) and wrestling. Eventually the games built up with the further introductions of boxing and equestrian events, including the very prestigious four horse chariot race and even races in armour. When the games

Olympia station stirs only at the arrival of a train

The Judas trees paint Olympia purple in spring

became too large to be completed by dusk they were extended into the following days and they were truly panhellenic, open to all whose native tongue was Greek. So that all could attend, and there was virtually continuous warring in the various regions, a truce was strictly enforced and observed for the period of the games. It was clearly obeyed because the games continued with the utmost regularity. Male competitors only were allowed in the stadium and they, and their trainers, were obliged to demonstrate their sex by competing in the nude.

The prize for success at the games was nothing more than a garland of wild olive but it immortalised the victor and his family. Such was the prestige of the games that the wealth of the sanctuaries steadily accumulated and treasuries were built to accept the votive offerings from the various Greek states. The Romans were eventually accepted and admitted to the games which, after reaching new heights of professionalism, ended under the ban of Emperor Theodosius in AD393.

Excavation of the site by the Germans started in 1875 and lasted for a period of 6 years but there have been further excavations since, notably 1936-41 and 1952. All the finds are located in the excellent museum in the town. A consequence of the excavations was the eventual revival of the games; the first modern Olympiad being held in Athens in 1896.

Within a few minutes walk from the centre of the village, the site lies in a silvan setting below Mount Kronos. In mid April, it takes on a haze of purple brilliance under the blossom of the Judas trees which flourish there. Things to see are:

The Palaistra: This square building from the third century BC, on the left after entering, was of uncertain purpose. It was either for wrestling and boxing or simply a meeting place. Some of its Doric columns have been restored but originally there were colonnades on all four sides.

The Temple of Hera: Both this temple and the Temple of Zeus lie within the Altis, a sacred area reserved for gods. It is a square area bounded on three sides by walls whose lines only can now be traced. The Doric Temple of Hera is the oldest temple on the site built around 600BC on foundations which are even earlier. The earlier wooden columns were replaced by stone in various styles. Four columns have been restored and there are several partial columns in place.

The Temple of Zeus: Built by Libon of Elis and completed around 457BC, this Doric style temple was one of the largest in Greece. In spite of the sixth-century earthquake, the foundations and many of the column bases and capitals survived allowing some restoration. Similarities with the Parthenon in Athens suggest that the same architect, Pheidias, may have been involved with the design.

Nymphaion Fountain: This semicircular fountain, close to the Temple of Hera, was built by the Athenian Herodes Atticus around AD160.

Treasuries: Lying adjacent to the fountain towards the stadium and built on a terrace overlooking the Altis, the treasuries were in effect small temples built by various cities to house their votive offerings.

The Stadium: In spite of all that is fine on the site, this is the biggest attraction to many visitors. The stadium as it is presently seen is the result of excavations and restoration by the German Archaeological Society in 1961-2 to its fourth-century form. There was no seating, only earth embankments to seat some forty thousand spectators and the starting and finishing lines can still be seen.

 The **Archaeological Museum** is housed in a modern building at the far end of the car park which is opposite the archaeological site. A prior visit to this excellent museum is worthwhile if only to see the scale model of the site which helps with locating the various buildings and visualising Olympia as it was in a late stage of its development. The excavations unearthed a treasure of finds from helmets and shields through to votive offerings, most of which are now housed in chronological order in the museum. Amongst many fine exhibits, one highlight is the sculptures from the Temple of Zeus in the central hall. The sculpture from the east pediment is thought to commemorate the chariot race between King Oinomaos and Pelops.

A history of the olympic games in memorabilia is in the Museum of Olympic Games located to the rear of the village on the west side.

Tour 4 • The Scenic Inland Route To The North Coast (105km/65 miles)

This drive through the mountains is as scenic and as varied as any in the Peloponnese. At the end awaits one of the great little train journeys of the world; the Kalavrita-Diakopto rack and pinion railway. Road surfaces are generally good and the section from Tripotama through Aroania, a non-classified road, is asphalted and good although some widening work is in progress in parts. Even taken slowly, the journey is easily accomplished in half a day.

Leave Olympia by heading east past the archaeological site in the direction of Tripoli. Just over a kilometre past the site entrance turn left following signs to Lambia (40km/25 miles) which leads straight away through the village of Miraka. A slow and steady climb leads through pine filled hollows and hillocks towards the distant mountains.

Beyond the village of Lala, which ribbons its way along the main road, pear trees dot the fertile plains and deciduous oak takes over from the pine. At the T-junction turn right towards Lambia and Tripoli. Scrubland dominates the hills with steadily decreasing height and, as trees seek refuge in the sheltered valleys, the terrain looks increasingly barren. **Lambia**, scattered around and down the hillside, has the charm of old wrought iron balconied houses and flocks of long haired woolley sheep. Kalavrita (50km/31 miles) appears on the signpost as a left turn at the next village, **Tripotama**, and from here the road follows through a long, broad river valley which is lush and green with crops of maize, wheat and vines. The tree-lined village of **Aroania**, festooned over the mountainside, marks the end of the valley and from here the road climbs into the mountains and to an open vista of distant mountain tops. Go left on meeting the main road to follow a pastoral route between the hills. An avenue of trees finally announces Kalavrita.

Situated at the foot of the Mount Helmos range at an altitude of 750m (2,460ft), **Kalavrita** is favoured by cool mountain air which keeps it fresh throughout spring and pleasant in the summer months. It has a reasonable amount of accommodation in the way of hotels and rooms largely to serve the nearby ski resort on Mount Helmos. If the town has a modern look then it is largely on account of one particular day fixed indelibly in the town's history, 13 December 1943. On this day the occupying German troops massacred 1,436 males over 15 and burnt the town. The clock on the Metropolitan church stands permanently at 2.34pm, the time of the massacre. Expect remembrance but do not expect too much sadness. The town has come to terms with it in its own way, by wearing it openly and sharing it with all its visitors. The large white cross just outside the town, on the road up to the ski resort, is part of a simple but poignant memorial to those who died.

Just 6km (4 miles) to the south-west lies **Ag Lavra**, perhaps the most famous monastery in Greece. It was here on 21 March 1821 that Germanos, the Archbishop of Patras, raised the standard of revolt against the Turks which launched the War of Independence. It was destroyed by fire in 1943 at the hands of the Nazis but rebuilt later.

Skiing at the Mount Helmos ski resort comes to a close sometime in late March or early April. The peaks on the Aroania range are mighty, reaching as high as 2,341m (7,678ft), so the snow hangs around the tops until well into early into summer. If the road starts off without much promise, it is immediately wider and better surfaced beyond the village. Turn left for the ski resort at the junction reached about half way up. The whole of the 15km (9 mile) drive is

The Spectacular Vouraikos Railway

The rack and pinion railway which descends from **Kalavrita** through the spectacular Vouraikos Gorge down to **Diakopto** is not to be missed. The fact that a railway exists at all can only be attributed to a remarkable feat of engineering. The small train wends and twists through tunnels and over rocky ledges squeezing through the narrowest parts with only the river as close companion and descends the steepest gradients (1 in 7) with the help of its rack and pinion

Zaxlorou village and station on the Kalavrita line

Travel by rail through the Vouraikos Gorge

system. There are around four trains a day in each direction and while the 22km (14 mile) journey through the gorge is spectacular at any time, trips made close to noon have the advantage of better lighting from an overhead sun. The train has only two coaches, one in front of and one to the rear of the diesel engine, providing good viewing for all passengers. It is still worth booking a first class (single or return) for the opportunity to sit in the small compartments at the extreme front or rear for this 1 hour journey. With a first class return fare costing barely more than the cost of a beer in Europe, this journey has to be the best value in Greece.

Kalavrita Railway Timetable Daily

dep. Kalavrita	09.06; 13.35; 16.26; 17.35
dep. Zaxloro	09.28; 13.57; 16.48; 17.57
arr. Diakopt	10.15; 14.45; 17.35; 18.44
dep. Diakopt	07.45; 10.42; 12.15; 15.08
dep. Zaxloro	08.30; 11.30; 13.03; 15.56
arr. Kalavrita	08.54; 11.51; 13.24; 16.17

The Vouraikos Railway meanders through tunnels and over rocky ledges

scenic but the real rewards are at the top with superb alpine views and a host of rare alpine flowers. The road ahead at the junction mentioned leads on to caves at the village of **Kastria**. Commercialisation of the caves is a recent development and road construction should now allow access. According to tourist office information, a narrow passage leads first into a small cave which broadens into an enormous cavern fully 2km (1 mile) long with fifteen miniature lakes formed by natural rock formations and attended by impressive displays of stalactites and stalagmites.

Moni Mega Spileo, the Monastery of the Great Cave, lies 6½km (4 miles) north of Kalavrita by the road down to Diakopto and can just as easily be visited by car as on foot. The monastery, built against a near vertical rock face utilising a cave, has early beginnings but it has suffered serious fires on a number of occasions. The last time was in 1934 when it was blown up by a barrel of gunpowder left over from the War of Independence. Its reconstruction in modern style is not so endearing. Once an important place of pilgrimage throughout the Middle Ages, it became one of the richest monasteries in Greece and possesses many old ikons. Visitors are usually shown around by a monk.

The Pine Processionary Caterpillar

The nests seen dripping from pine trees both here and along many of the Mediterranean coasts in Greece are full of the Pine Processionary Caterpillar (*Thaumetopoea pityocampa*). They live in these communal nests through the winter and come out to feed only when the weather is warm enough. Their communal behaviour persists even on leaving the nest and they move in procession, each one in contact nose to tail with the next to form chains extending to several metres in length. When fully grown, which is usually by late spring or early summer, they pupate in cocoons below ground and emerge as moths later in the summer. Eggs are laid in large numbers around the pine needles and are covered by scales from the body of the female. The reproductive cycle is completed in the course of one year.

A word of warning; these dark brown caterpillars are covered in hairs which are highly irritant and will cause a painful rash if they come into contact with the skin.

Tour 5 • Back To Athens

There are choices to make for the return to Athens. The first route is the most direct whilst the second takes advantage of the ferry between Rio and Andirio to cross the Gulf of Corinth and include Delphi in the itinerary.

Route 1 : Kalavrita • Diakopto • Corinth • Athens (205km/127 miles)

The first stage descends to the coast at Diakopto and then there is a choice of either joining the fast road, which passes as motorway, or continuing along the old coast road as far as Corinth. The latter is easily the most scenic run and fairly free flowing although some heavies still use the route. For the final leg from Corinth to Athens, the toll road is the better option.

Route 2 : Kalavrita • Diakopto • Rio • Andirio • Delphi (198km/123 miles) • Levadia • Thiva • Athens (364km/226 miles)

For travellers with time in hand, this route offers the opportunity to see Delphi on the return without too much extra mileage. Details of Delphi and other places of interest en route back to Athens as well as additional tours in the northern mainland are described in the *Visitor's Guide to Greece* published by Moorland Publishing and also written by Brian and Eileen Anderson.

Road conditions are good throughout and the ferry crossings are frequent, inexpensive and require only 20 minutes sea time. After descending from Kalavrita to Diakopto, the coastal road westwards to Rio is pleasing to drive and rewarding for its fine scenery over the gulf. A good, fast road from Andirio skims along the coast for much of the way revealing occasional glimpses of attractive little bays. One such bay, at Skalana, just after Nafpaktos, makes an ideal picnic spot.

Zaxlorou To Moni Mega Spileo On Foot

Apart from a halt just outside Kalavrita, Zaxlorou is the one and only station on the line down to Diakopto and the journey time is around 25 minutes. From the tiny and isolated village Zaxlorou which seems only a taverna and a clutch of houses bigger than the station, there is an old trail which leads up to join the main road just below the Monastery of Mega Spileo. The way is constantly uphill and the footpaths are often very stony. It takes around 45 minutes to reach the monastery from the station and much the same to return.

Alight at Zaxlorou and walk past the front of the hotel and taverna to join the path which continues alongside the gorge rising steadily. Very shortly there are good views looking backwards to the station but, soon afterwards, the path starts to wind to the left, up the side of the gorge and away from the railway line. The slow, steady uphill pace at least leaves time to appreciate the wild flowers by the wayside which in April includes the dwarf iris-like flowers (*Hermodactylus tuberosus*) and the *Anemone blanda*. The road is reached in around 30 minutes and the monastery can now be clearly seen up to the left. From here the route to it follows along the road.

Additional Information

Places to Visit

Arcadia
Castle
The castle is unguarded with free access.

Methoni
Castle
Open: daily, including Sundays and holidays, 9pm-3pm.

Nestor's Palace
Site and Museum (at Hora)
Open: daily, iencluding Sundays and holidays, 8.30pm-3pm. Closed on Monday.

Olympia
Site
Open: 8am-7pm Monday to Friday and 8.30am-3pm on Saturday and Sunday.

Olympia Museum
Open: 11.30am-6pm on Monday 8am-7pm Tuesday to Friday and 8am-3pm on Saturday and Sunday.

Olympic Games Museum
Open: 8pm-3.30pm Monday to Saturday and 9am-4.30pm on Sunday.

Pylos
Neokastro
Open: daily 8.30pm-3pm. Closed
on Monday.

Accommodation

HOTELS
* = Open all year

ANDRITSENA: TELEPHONE PREFIX 0626
Hotel Theoxenia (B)
☎ 22219/35/70

Hotel Pan (D)

Arcadia
Karitena has no hotel but there are
private rooms available.

Finikounda: TELEPHONE PREFIX 0723
Hotel Finikounda* (C)
☎ 71208/71308/71408

Hotel Porto Finissia* (C)
☎ 71358/71457/71458

KALAMATA: TELEPHONE PREFIX 0721
Hotel Elite* (A)
2 Navarinou ☎ 25015/22434/85303

Hotel Rex* (B)
26 Aristomenous
☎ 22334/23291-4

Hotel Flisvos* (C)
135 Navarinou
☎ 82282/82177

Hotel Valassis* (C)
95 Navarinou
☎ 23849/25751

KALAVRITA: TELEPHONE PREFIX 0692
Hotel Filoxenia* (B)
☎ 22422/22290/22493

Hotel Helmos (B)
Eletherias Square
☎ 22217

Villa Kalavrita
Rooms and suites
☎ 22712/22845

KARDAMILI: TELEPHONE PREFIX 0721
Hotel Kalamitsi (B) ☎ 73131

Karamili Beach*
Hotel & Bungalows (C)
☎ 73180/84

Hotel Pariarcheas (C) ☎ 73366

KORONI: TELEPHONE PREFIX 0725
Auberge de la Plage, pension (B)
☎ 0725 22401

MESSINI: TELEPHONE PREFIX 0722
Hotel Messini* (C)
Pilou Ave
☎ 23002/3

Hotel Drossia* (C)
20 Dariotou
☎ 23248/22457

Hotel Lyssandros* (C)
☎ 22921/24336

METHONI: TELEPHONE PREFIX 0723
Hotel Odysseas* (B) ☎ 31600
Hotel Alex* (C) ☎ 31219/31245
Pension Methoni Beach*(B) ☎ 31544/5

OLYMPIA: TELEPHONE PREFIX 0624
Hotel Amalia* (A) ☎ 22190/1
Hotel Antonios* (A) ☎ 22348/9
Hotel Altis (B) ☎ 23101/2

Hotel Apollon (B)
13 Douma ☎ 22522/22513

Hotel Neda* (B)
1 K. Karamanli ☎ 22563/22692

Hotel New Olympia (B) ☎ 22547/22506
Hotel Artemis (C) 2 Tsoureka ☎ 22255
Hotel Hercules* (C) ☎ 22696/22532
Hotel Inomaos* (C) ☎ 22056
Hotel Pelops* (C) 2 Varela ☎ 22543

PYLOS: TELEPHONE PREFIX **0723**
*Hotel Miramare** (B) ☎ 22226/22751

*Hotel Karalis** (C)
26 Kalamatas ☎ 22960/22980

*Hotel Galaxy** (C)
Trion Navaron Square
☎ 22780/22784

*Pension Karalis Beach** (B) ☎ 23021/2

STOUPA: TELEPHONE PREFIX **0721**
Hotel Halikoura Beach (C) ☎ 54303
Hotel Lefktro (C) ☎ 54322
Hotel Stoupa (C) ☎ 54308

CAMPING
* = Open all year
The sites listed here open April/
May through until September/
October.

Finikounda
Ammos ☎ 0723 71262/71333

Kardamili
Melitzina ☎ 0721 73461 or Athens 01
6513420

Koroni
Koroni Camping ☎ 0725 22119

Memi Beach
☎ 0725 22130 or Athens 01 2523406

Methoni
Camping ☎ 0723 31228

Olympia
Alfios, Drouva Arch ☎ 0624 22950/2
Diana (open all year)
Ancient Olympia ☎ 0624 22314/22425
Olympia Beach ☎ 0624 22738/22745

Pylos
Navarino
Gialova ☎ 0273 22761

Petalidi
Petalidi Beach ☎ 0722 31154

Sun Beach
Petalidi ☎ 0722 31200/31110 or
Athens 01 8171406

Stoupa
Kalogria ☎ 0721 54319/54327

Transport

MESSINIA: Kalamata, as capital of
the region, is well connected to
Athens. There are daily flights
from the airport which lies just
outside Kalamata towards Messini
as well as bus and train services.
The trains, around 5 daily, run via
Kiparissia and Patra for a journey
time of 7½ hours. The buses, some
10 daily, use a more direct route
which takes about 4½ hours.

Locally, there are fairly frequent
bus services out of Kalamata to
destinations such as Messini, Pylos,
Olympia, Gythio and Areopolis.
From Pylos connections to Athens
are limited, two buses daily, but
there is a better service to Methoni.

ILIA: Olympia is well served by bus
to Athens and to many centres in
the Peloponnese including Tripoli,
Argos, Sparti, Megalopolis, Karitena,
Andritsena, Kalamata and Nafplio.
In addition is has also a rail service
with daily trains to Patras, Corinth
Athens, Piraeus, Pirgos, Kalamata
and Argos.

Tourist Information Centres

Ilia
Municipality Information Office
Praxitelous Kondili
Olympia
☎ 0624 231125/23100/23173

Messinia
Municipality Information Office
221 Kalamata 24100
☎ 0721 22059/21959

Greece: Fact File

Accommodation

Hotels

These are classified by the National Tourist Office of Greece (NTOG—EOT when in Greece) into De Luxe, AA and A class which are subject to a minimum price structure only. Bars, restaurants and swimming pools are the facilities that you expect to find, but the class in itself is not a guarantee of the standard of service. Mostly, higher grade hotels are found in cities and in regions where there is a demand.

In addition there are B, C and D classes for which the room rates are fixed by the NTOG. These hotels are obliged to display their category and price of each room. There is no C in the Greek alphabet so this class is represented by the gamma sign 'G.' Extra charges described as taxes or service may be added to the final rate. Note that the charge is a room charge, not a charge per person and may or may not include breakfast. Room charges are seasonal with low, mid and high season rates. It is possible to bargain, especially for 3 days or more, but you are most likely to succeed out of high season. Generally the C class hotels have rooms with bathrooms as do many of the D class but here it is not obligatory. Away from big cities, these hotels are often family run and offer a good level of cleanliness and comfort. The lower grade hotels may not have bar or restaurant facilities, except for breakfast.

The Tourist Office itself runs a chain of Xenia Hotels (A, B & C class) scattered throughout the country which are often delightfully situated.

Pensions

Accommodation of this kind in small hotels or private houses can also be very good. Again, the standards are controlled and graded by the NTOG but take each one on its own merit and inspect before you commit yourself. At best they are very good with private bathroom facilities.

Villas and Apartments

There are many scattered around popular tourist locations. Many are in the hands of letting agencies who place them with tour operators. One technique for searching them out is to read through the holiday brochures of companies who specialise in this type of accommodation. Many of these villas are often not in use until late May or early June, so it is possible to make private arrangements on the spot, sometimes at very attractive rates.

Rooms
In the main tourist areas, there are generally plenty of private houses offering rooms at budget rates. If you arrive in Greece by ferry, the chances are that you will be met at the dockside by a cluster of 'Room to Let' notices, otherwise enquire at the local NTOG office or with the Tourist Police.

Traditional Settlements
This is a recent development organised by the NTOG in which old houses have been restored in their original architecture but now with modern facilities. At present there are three locations in the Peloponnese and locations are given in the appropriate chapters. Reservations can be made at the NTOG head office in Athens and further details can be obtained from NTOG offices.

Camping
Camping in areas other than on official camping grounds is not permitted in any part of the country. It is something which the Greek authorities are strict on, especially in popular tourist regions. However, there are now camp sites for both caravans and tents, often set in attractive locations. Standards vary, some are well equipped with modern facilities and are open all year round. Other sites are run by the NTOG and the rates for all the services are fixed. Further details from: Association of Greek Camping, 102 Solonos Street, 10680 Athens ☎ 362 1560

Banks

Banks are open Monday to Thursday 8am-2pm. Friday 8am-1.30pm, so money should be changed in a morning.

In large cites and in popular tourist locations, certain banks may open for a short period in the late afternoon. The best place for changing money in Athens outside the accepted banking hours or at weekend is the National Bank of Greece, 2 Karageorgi Serias Street. Open: Monday to Thursday 8am-2pm & 3.30-6.30pm. Friday 8am-1.30pm & 3-6.30pm. Saturday 9am-3pm. Sunday 9am-1pm.

Some banks now have automatic cash dispensers which will

Average Daily Temperatures

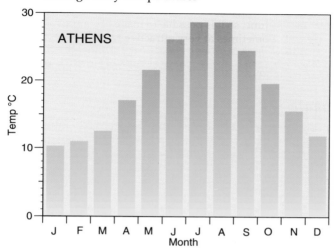

Average Monthly Rainfall

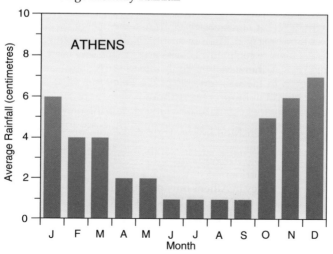

accept Eurocheque cards. Oddly enough, foreign services are not always available through these tills on National Holidays when most needed!

The only round the clock banking service, 7 days a week, at the Agricultural Bank of Greece at East Air Terminal (International). At West Air Terminal, the National Bank of Greece is open 7am-11pm, 7 days a week.

Climate

Spring is in the air as early as March but the temperatures do not start to rise significantly until April and May. In coastal regions both these months are fresh and warm enough for shorts on sunny days, but still with a risk of the odd rainy day. The region has a Mediterranean climate which means mild, wet winters and hot, dry summers. Thus there are plenty of rainy days in the winter months but becoming dry through April and May with summer rain largely confined to short thunder storms. The mountain regions are much colder in winter, often with snow on the high peaks, and slightly cooler in summer with a higher risk of rainy days.

June sees the temperatures warming steadily towards summer heat with the evenings and nights becoming warmer too. Throughout July, August into September it is hot by day and by night. It seems much easier to sleep in the heat of the day than in the night-time heat. The days are made more bearable by the wind, the Meltemi, which blows incessantly, rising and fading with the sun. However, the Meltemi only affects the eastern half and does not reach to the western side of the Peloponnese. It feels much more humid in those areas without it.

High summer is not the best time for touring unless you stay in the mountain areas where the temperatures are still high but the air feels fresher and cooler in the evening.

Sometime, usually late in September, a short unsettled spell brings an end to the summer heat. Temperatures fall significantly and the air feels fresh again. Good weather continues through October into November but with an ever increasing risk of rainy days. The risk of rain is higher in the mountain regions.

This describes an average pattern which is not the same as a forecast. The summer is reliably hot but there can be a fair variation from the norm in spring and autumn.

Crime and Theft

The incidence of crime and theft is rising in Athens and other cities but it is still at a relatively low level. There is no need to feel threatened, even in the evening but it is sensible to be cautious late at night, especially women on their own.

Many hotels have safety deposit boxes available for guests at a small charge. Otherwise, keep valuables out of sight. This is particularly true if you have a car. Cameras, personal stereos and the like are best carried with you but if you need to leave them in the car make sure they are locked in the boot.

If you are unfortunate enough to suffer a loss then report it to the Tourist Police by dialling 171.

If your loss includes a passport then you will need to contact your Embassy. See page 134.

Currency & Credit Cards

Foreign currency in excess of $1,000 US or more than 100,000 Greek *drachma* must be declared on entry. Failure to comply may result in fines or confiscation. There is no limit on gold or gold coins.

Tourists can take out of Greece up to 20,000 *drachma* plus foreign currencies up to $1,000 US. Higher amounts are allowed if there has been an import declaration.

Money Matters

The local currency is the *drachma* which is indicated by drx or simply Dx (DR) before the number. *Drachma* notes commonly in circulation include 5,000, 1,000, 500, 100 and 50 with coins of 50, 20, 10 ,5, 2 and 1 *drachma* value.

Travellers cheques, Eurocheques and hard currencies are freely accepted at banks, Post Offices and Exchange Bureaus. Major credit cards and charge cards are also widely accepted in hotels, shops and restaurants in the large cities. In provincial regions, their use is mostly restricted to hotels and sometimes to only the larger ones. When driving in the countryside, do not count on credit cards to pay for fuel.

Although it is possible to get a cash advance on a credit card, there still seems to be some suspicion of this. Only certain banks co-operate and the best ones to try are the National Bank of Greece and the Commercial Bank. There is a minimum size of transaction, around 15,000 *drachma*.

Always take your passport when changing money. Even though the production of a passport may not be a requirement, the Greeks rely on them as a means of identification. You may even be asked for it when purchasing an internal flight ticket. In terms of commission, the cheapest place to change money is at a bank and the mostt expensive is usually the hotel reception.

Disabled Facilities

While there is an awareness of this problem, few practical steps have been taken to improve matters. Only the international hotels provide anything like adequate facilities. Street ramps are starting to appear in the main cities but in other places the pavements are non existent or barely fit for even the most able.

Embassies and Consulates

Foreign Embassies andConsulates in Greece are:

Australia
37 D Soutsou Street & An
Tsocha
115 21 Athens
☎ 6447303

Canada
4 I. Genadiou Street
115 21 Athens
☎ 7239511-9

New Zealand
15-17 Tsocha Street
115 21 Athens
☎ 6410311- 5

USA
Embassy-Consulate
91 Vass. Sophias Avenue
115 21 Athens
☎ 721951-9 & 7218 400

UK
Embassy-Consulate
1 Ploutarchou Street
106 75 Athens
☎ 7236211-19

Vice Consulate
45 Thessaloniki Street
Kavala
☎ (051) 223704

Vice Consulate
2 Votsi Street
Patra
☎ (061) 277329

Consulate
8 Venizelou Street
Eleftherias Square
Thessaloniki
☎ (031) 278006/269984

Electricity

Mains electricity in Greece is 220 volts AC with just a few rural districts still on 110 DC. Electrical equipment should be fitted with a continental two pin plug or an appropriate adapter used.

Greek Time

Greek normal time is 2 hours ahead of GMT. The clocks advance one hour for summertime starting the last Sunday in March and ending the last Sunday in September.

America and Canada: Greek normal time is ahead of time in America, 7 hours ahead of Eastern Standard, 8 hours ahead of Central, 9 hours ahead of Mountain and 10 hours ahead of Pacific Time.

Australia and New Zealand: Greek normal time is 7½ hours behind South Australia, 8 hours behind New South Wales, Tasmania and Victoria and 10 hours behind time in New Zealand. These differences relate to GMT but, to take into account clock changes for Daylight Saving hours, the following corrections should be made: add 1 hour to these differences from late September to the end of March and subtract 1 hour from late March to the end of September.

Health Care

For minor ailments like headaches or tummy upsets, head for the chemist shop (*farmakion*). If you need a further supply of prescription drugs make sure to take a copy of your prescription and the chances are that you will be able to get them. Most chemists, certainly in the large towns, speak English.

If it is a doctor or dentist you require, the chemist shop again should be able to assist. If that does not work then contact the Tourist Police. There are English speaking doctors and dentists in most large towns.

Problems really start if hospital treatment is required. European countries have reciprocal arrangements with the Greeks for free medical treatment, subject to certain restrictions. British visitors should take an E111 form obtained from the Post Offices. To operate the scheme you need to find the local Greek Social Insurance office (IKA) who, after inspecting your E111, will direct you to a registered doctor or dentist. If you are in a region remote from an IKA office then you must pay privately for your treatment and present your bills to an IKA official before you leave Greece. Up to half your costs may be refunded. The best answer is to ensure that you have adequate holiday insurance cover.

Emergency treatment, sunburn, broken bones etc, is free in state hospitals. But for treatment as an in patient, nursing care is restricted only to medical treatment and it is left to the family to supply general nursing care, drinks, food and even blankets. It is generally preferable to have private medical insurance.

Health Hazards

The sun is very burning even on a hazy day and great care is needed to protect from sunburn and sunstroke particularly at the start of your holiday. Sun creams help considerably but, at least for the first few days, take light clothing to cover up and control the exposure of your skin to the sun. A slowly acquired tan lasts longer.

Mosquitoes can be a nuisance in the evening and throughout the night. If you sit or dine outside in the evening, particularly near trees, either cover up your arms and legs or use insect repellent. An electric machine which slowly vaporises a pellet is very efficient, especially in a closed room. Anthisan cream is an effective treatment for bites, particularly if applied immediately.

Care is needed on the beach to avoid stings from jelly fish and, in rocky regions, from sea urchins. It is important to ensure that all the urchin spines are properly removed. Beach shoes will give your feet some protection from stings.

Stomach upsets are perhaps the most common ailment. The excess olive oil used in cooking and over salads can be a cause of this so take care with oily foods to start with. The digestive system adjusts within a few days and you can soon eat giant beans swimming in oil without fear. Squeeze plenty of fresh lemon over your food to counter the oil and, if still troubled, an acidic drink, like Coca-Cola, helps. Drinking wine to excess can cause similar symptoms. More serious are the upsets caused by bad water and bad food. Generally the water in Greece is good to drink but in high summer be more careful and use bottled water which is freely available. Avoiding food poisoning is not always possible but there are elementary precautions that can help. Most tavernas prepare cooked dishes for the lunch time and these are kept warm until finally sold. If they are still there in the evening, and they often are, avoid them. Ask for something which requires grilling or roasting.

When out in the hot sun it is essential to drink plenty of liquid, particularly water.

Holiday Insurance
Whichever holiday insurance you choose, make sure that the cover for medical expenses is more than adequate. It helps too if there is an emergency 24 hour contact to take care of arrangements, including repatriation if necessary. Injuries caused while taking part in certain hazardous pursuits are normally excluded from medical cover. Look carefully at the specified hazardous pursuits; in recent times, injuries caused by riding a moped or motor-bike have been added to the list by some insurers.

Language

Many Greeks speak good English, especially in the large towns and in tourist areas. Children learn it in state schools and most of them attend private schools as well. After all, English is the official second language in Greece and all official notices are presented in Greek and English, at least the more recent notices.

Some knowledge of the Greek language is not only useful to help you get by, but can enhance enormously the pleasure of your holiday. It is worthwhile getting a good phrase book and an audio tape to learn some simple Greek. The Greeks really warm to you if you make the slightest effort with their language.

Place Names
With no official transliteration, the latinisation of the Greek alphabet is open to various interpretations which leads to much confusion. The conversion of the double consonants, for example, is one cause of difficulty. The Greek mp is pronounced as b at the start of a word but mb in the middle. A Greek word starting with mp is almost invariably Latinised to begin with b but in the middle of the word both mp and mb can be observed. The Vale of Tempe is also seen as the Vale of Tembi. Vowel sounds, especially e and i, do not always strictly correspond so there is a tendency to substitute the more phonetically correct, as in Tembi, the last example. Some single consonants have no strict equivalent either, such as X, pronounced as the ch in loch, and this is Latinised to ch, which is

a mile away phonetically, or h which is a little better. The village of Xora appears as Chora or Hora. All these difficulties are reflected in the spelling of place names. Pick up three different maps and it is more than likely that many of the same villages will have three different spellings. This book uses the spelling observed on the sign outside the village or, since many villages are without name boards, the spelling which leads to a more accurate pronunciation.

Luggage

Since Greece is a full member of the EEC all leading brands of food and products are freely available with national peculiarities. As the Greeks do not normally start the day with breakfast, only a limited range of breakfast cereals can be bought in some popular tourist regions. If you have a favourite brand of tea or tea bags then it is easy to find room for some in your luggage. If you are self catering it is wise to take teacloths and rubbish bags with you.

There are a few other items which are worth considering if only to save time shopping when you are there:

A universal sink plug — this is useful when travelling.

An electric mosquito repeller and tablets are readily available in Greece, but small 'travel' types are a convenient size for packing and will last for years. Make sure you buy one with a continental 2 pin plug.

Insect repellent — if you prefer a particular brand, buy it at home.

Other useful items are a compact folding umbrella, particularly if you are visiting Greece outside the main season. Rain showers tend to be short and, with the rain falling straight down, an umbrella gives good protection, better than a waterproof which can quickly make you hot and sweaty. A small rucksack is useful too, not just for if you go walking, but for general use when heading for the beach or off on a shopping trip. Walkers, and even motorists, should take a plastic water bottle. It is important to carry water when walking in a hot climate and it is difficult to buy a plastic bottle in Greece which does not leak.

It is rarely necessary to take a heavy jumper but it is always useful to take some thinner layers of clothing which you can wear together. Sometimes it is cool in the evening or you may feel cool after the heat of the sun. If you intend to do any serious walking,

walking on country tracks as opposed to city streets, make sure you have suitable footwear.

Most basic medical requirements, plasters, bandages, headache pills can be bought in chemist shops in Greece. More than that, many drugs normally available in Britain only on prescription can be bought over the counter on demand and at reasonable prices.

Note that codeine and drugs containing codeine are strictly banned in Greece so be sure to exclude these from your luggage.

Maps

Road maps of Greece may look good, but accuracy is something they are careful to avoid. The main trunk roads are reliably marked but the position of joining roads does not necessarily relate to reality. Signposts, if there are any at all, are placed immediately on junctions, making navigation incovenient. This situation is improving and major routes are better in this respect. Road numbers have recently been changed so do not always correspond to those on earlier maps. To add to the confusion there are still too many roads which, for reasons not even to be guessed at, do not appear on road maps. The map of Greece supplied by the Greek National Tourist Office is as accurate as any.

Newspapers & Magazines

The *Financial Times*, most British newspapers, a selection from European countries and the *Herald Tribune* are usually available in large towns and centres of tourism. Mostly they are one day late and sometimes more. Expect a fair mark up in price. The place to look for newspapers is at the kiosks (*periptera*) where they are displayed on racks or along the counter, or in book shops which are generally few and far between.

Also available throughout Greece on the day of issue is the English language *Athens News*. It contains local and international stories, an entertainment section announcing local events and concerts, sport and TV listings. *Greek Weekly News*, more competently produced, full of interest and with a good listing of events and concerts, is published on Saturday evening.

A selection of English and European magazines is also available, again at the *periptera*. The best locally produced English language magazine is *The Athenian* which appears monthly, and is also useful for its comprehensive listings of cultural events.

Passports & Visas

EEC nationals should not require a passport but still do.

Nationals from USA, Australia, Canada, New Zealand, Norway, Sweden, Finland and certain other nations require only a valid passport for a stay of up to 3 months in Greece. For a stay exceeding 3 months, it is necessary to register at the Aliens Department which, in Athens, is located at: 173 Alexandras Avenue, 115 22 Athens ☎ 646 8103/770 5711 ext 379.

Local police forces too have an Aliens Department outside. Athens you can report locally to obtain an extension. The whole process is long and drawn out, often requiring 2 to 3 weeks or more, and you will be asked to provide up to 6 passport-size photographs. These are worth taking with you if you plan a long stay. In addition you will be asked to show visible means of support, ie a good number of money exchange slips. If convenient, one option is to leave the country briefly, preferably overnight, and return making sure that you get a passport stamp on re-entry. You may wish to plead ignorance of the requirements and opt to pay the fine when you leave the country which is quite small, roughly equalling the duties you would have paid for an extended visa.

Pets

Cats and dogs require health and rabies inoculation certificates issued by a veterinary authority in the country of origin not more than 12 months (cats 6 months) and not less than 6 days prior to arrival.

Photography

Signs with a camera crossed out indicate a prohibited area for photography. Notices of this kind are posted near every military establishment, no matter how small or insignificant. Disregard this at your peril. The Greeks are paranoiac about security and anyone found using a camera in a prohibited zone faces unpleasant consequences. The photographer is normally held in custody while the film is developed and inspected. It could mean overnight detention.

Photography on archaeological sites is free but if you use a tripod without the insertion of a live subject then a fee is demanded. Photography with a camera mounted on a tripod is prohibited in museums and moving pictures are subject to a fee according to the category.

Outdoors, the light for photography is brilliant. Summer haze can cause difficulties with distant shots but the use of a UV or skylight filter is helpful here. Some of the clearest days occur in spring when a cool north wind blows. Mid-day light is harsh and contrasty, mornings and evening provide the best lighting conditions for serious photography.

Places to Visit

Ancient Sites and Monasteries
Most of the ancient sites are fenced off and there is an entrance fee to look around. Opening and closing times vary from site to site but for all the major sites these are given in the text or at the end of each chapter. Do not count on being able to buy site guides at all sites, sometimes only glossy books are sold. If your interest runs deeper than the information given in this book, the best advice is to go equipped with your own guide.

Students can claim reduced fees on production of a student's card.

Archaeological sites are closed on certain public holidays which include 1 January, 25 March, Good Friday and Easter Monday, 1 May and 25 & 26 December.

Museums
There is a charge for admission. Opening and closing times vary but most, not all, close on a Monday. Refer to the appropriate chapter for further details.

Museums are closed, or open only for a short while, on the public holidays listed under ancient sites. In addition they have half-days on Shrove Monday, Whitsunday, 15 August, 28 October and Epiphany, 6 January.

Postal Services

Post Offices are open only on weekdays 7.30am-2pm. They are closed on Saturday and Sunday. The exceptions are the Athens Post Offices in Syntagma Square, Omonia Square and Acropolis which also open Sundays 9am-1.30pm and the mobile Post Office in Monastiraki Square which is open weekdays 8am-6pm and on Sundays 8am-6pm.

Stamps (*grammatosima*) can be purchased at Post Offices, sometimes at a special counter, or at some kiosks (*periptera*).

Letters from Greece to overseas destinations are delivered fairly speedily, 4-6 days for Europe, 6-8 for USA and longer for Australia and New Zealand. For a speedier delivery, ask for express post on which there is a fairly modest surcharge but it cuts 2-3 days off the delivery time.

Post cards take forever, or so it seems, especially at peak holiday times. Even to nearby Europe they regularly take 2 weeks which often means you arrive home before the cards you sent. Cards go at the same postal rate as letters so slip a card inside an airmail envelope and post it as a letter. It leaves more space on the card for writing too. Envelopes (*fakellos*) can be bought very cheaply at stationers.

Public Holidays and Festivals

The Greek calendar overflows with public holidays, Saints days and festivals. On public holidays, banks shops and offices are closed although restaurants and tavernas normally stay open.

Public transport is often interrupted too, reverting either to a Sunday service or none at all. Filling stations also close for many of the holidays. These holidays are:

1 January — New Year's Day
6 January — Epiphany
25 March — Independence Day
Monday before Lent — Clean Monday
April — Good Friday & Easter Monday
1 May — May Day
15 August — Assumption of the Blessed Virgin Mary
28 October — Ochi Day
25 December — Christmas Day
26 December — Boxing Day

Easter is variable and does not always coincide with Easter throughout the rest of Europe. Accommodation can be a problem at this time so either book in advance or head for a major resort which caters for tourists.

Name-days are one reason why the calendar is so full of celebrations. It has been a long tradition for Greeks to ignore birthdays and to celebrate instead the special day of their saint, and there are a lot of saints. If you see people wandering around with cake boxes neatly tied with fancy ribbon, or bunches of flowers or unusual activity around one of the many churches, then the chances are that it is a name-day. The custom is for the person celebrating to offer hospitality to friends, to neighbours and to almost anyone who will partake of a little ouzo and refreshments.

Some of the important name days are:

23 April — St George's day
All Georges everywhere celebrate their special day but in addition to that it is also the national day of Greece
21 May — Saints Konstantinos and Eleni
15 August — Assumption of the Blessed Virgin Mary
This is the day when millions of Marias celebrate and an important day in the religious calendar often marked by local pilgrimages or festivals
8 November for all Michaels and Gabriels
6 December — Feast of St Nicholas

Easter is the biggest and the most important celebration of the year. The arrival of Carnival time commences the long build up. This festival takes place throughout the 3 weeks before Lent and may commence as early as late January. Fancy dress is an important part of the tradition. It arises from the period of Turkish occupation when Greeks were banned from conducting these celebrations. Driven under-cover, festivities continued with people disguised to prevent recognition. Now it is firmly rooted into the custom and costumes are worn at all events. Children wander the streets in fancy dress and traditionally show defiance by wearing their disguises on the last school day of Carnival.

All this comes to an abrupt end with a complete change of mood on 'Clean Monday' (Kathari Deutera), the Monday before Lent. This is a public holiday when families traditionally exodus to the country, which mostly means heading to a taverna. Special meat-free menus are the order of the day.

Lent is still strictly observed by many, especially in country regions. Serious preparations for Easter start on Maundy Thursday. Shoppers buy eggs, not by the tens but by the hundreds. The rest of the day is spent in boiling the eggs and dying them red, which is supposed to have protective powers and the first egg dyed belongs to the Virgin.

Good Friday is a day of complete fast and widely observed. In large towns there are usually some tavernas open but in country areas it can be difficult or impossible to find food. The sombre mood of the day is heightened by the continual tolling of church bells. It is a day for remembering their own dead; graves are visited and wreaths are laid. In the evening, the burial of Christ is the most moving and widely attended service in the Greek Orthodox calendar. Cafés and tavernas close and there is not one Greek who would willingly miss the candle-lit procession and service.

Saturday brings an air of expectancy. In dimly lit churches everywhere, services begin. Slowly the light intensity increases reaching full brightness at midnight when priests triumphantly chant 'Christ is risen'. Light from the priest's candle is passed to the congregation and that flame is passed from candle to candle until it reaches the crowds outside. Fire crackers drown the clamour of the church bells. The crowds disperse shortly carefully protecting their burning candle; it is a good omen to enter the home with the flame still burning.

Sunday is a day of rejoicing, with a spit-roast lamb or, in some areas, goat. The red eggs now appear and are used in friendly competition. Each contestant taps their egg hard enough to break an opponent's but not their own.

Easter Monday has no special ceremonies or rituals and passes as any normal public holiday.

Cultural Events

In addition to the major festivals listed with each chapter, local festivals are commonplace in the summer months. A word of warning too. Each town and village has its own saint's day and sometimes, depending on the local whim and the phase of the moon, a holiday is called. This decision is often not taken until the day before so there is no way you can plan for such eventualities.

Public Toilets

The most usual sign is WC with figures to indicate ladies (*gynaikon*) and gents (*andron*). Toilets with permanent attendants who demand a fee, usually found in the larger towns and cities, are normally quite clean but others can be appalling. There are also toilets in museums and at archaeological sites. Toilet paper is sometimes supplied where there is an attendant and very occasionally elsewhere. Take your own supply.

Public Transport

Buses

Buses throughout Greece are mainly operated by a syndicate of privately owned companies operating under the name of KTEL. They operate a vast network and their faded green and cream buses can be seen cruising along main roads or struggling through clouds of dust to some mountain village. Mainline buses, often air conditioned, are efficiently run and mostly leave promptly from their starting point. Tickets for these buses are often bought from an office at the terminal immediately before the journey. Tickets bought this way often have a seat number which is the number on the reverse of the seat on which you sit and not the number you sit facing. Although this is a logical system once it is understood, it takes only a few inexperienced travellers to reduce a bus to chaos within minutes. When a ticket service is not operating, or if you join at an intermediate point, pay the driver on entry. Local services or those on short runs mostly operate with a conductor to collect fares.

In moderate size towns, there may be two or more bus stations; local buses using one and long distance buses the others, according to destinations.

The State Railway Organisation, OSE, also operates an express bus service between major cities. They depart from railway stations and their charges are similar to KTEL.

Details of bus services in Athens are given at the end of Chapter 1.

Trains

The railway network is not so extensive and the trains are generally slow compared to the buses, but they are cheaper. Trains usually have some first-class compartments, although the standards are not significantly better than second class. It is possible to reserve a seat in either class, and at no extra charge, but only if you join the train at the starting point.

For a spectacular journey, try the rack and pinion line in the Peloponnese between Diakopto and Kalavrita. See Chapter 4 for more details.

Taxis

Taxis are relatively cheap and well used in Greece. In the cities it is fairly straightforward. All licensed taxis are designated by a roof

145

sign and fitted with a meter which displays the fare in *drachmas*. The rate of charges and surcharges are fixed. Within the city boundaries taxi fares are charged at the single rate and you may see 1 displayed in a solitary box on the meter. Once you travel outside the city boundary, the double rate applies so it is likely you will see the driver alter the meter so that 2 shows in the box. Legitimate small surcharges are allowed for a sizeable piece of luggage, for attending an airport, port or station for the benefit of passengers, and for late night or very early morning travel. Surcharges are permitted too at holiday times, especially Christmas and Easter. Picking up a second fare is allowed too so you may find yourself sharing a taxi.

Most of the licensed taxi drivers are good and honest but there are always a few who regard tourists as a good source of revenue. Some of the tricks encountered include: the meter does not work, the meter set on the double rate when it should be single and, worst of all, multiplying the charge by ten which is easily done by wrongly reading the display on the modern digital meter.

Avoid unlicensed cabs where at all possible. These are not fitted with a meter and their charges can be extortionate. At the ports and airports, drivers of these cabs tend to stalk their prey on foot offering their taxi service. Obligingly, help will be offered with your luggage and you will be hustled into the cab. There will be hardly time to notice that it is an unofficial cab.

If you intend to travel a distance outside the city centre, it is common practice to negotiate your fare with the driver before you start the journey. Do not hesitate to ask two or three drivers for a quote on the fare, it is the only yardstick available.

One last word of warning, for a period of around 3 hours, between 2pm and 5pm (siesta time), it can be almost impossible to get a taxi, particularly in Athens.

Recorded Information

Time ☎ 141
Weather ☎ 148
News ☎ 115
Buses (Greece) ☎ 142
Ships (Piraeus, Rafina, Lavrio) ☎ 143
Trains (Greece) ☎ 145
Trains (Europe) ☎ 147
Road assistance (ELPA) ☎ 104

Shopping

Regulations on opening hours have changed recently to adjust to market needs. Different regions have their own views on this so there is now greater confusion than ever over opening times. Big city supermarkets and department stores open: Monday-Friday 8am-8pm; Saturday 8am-3pm.

Pharmacies: Monday and Wednesday 8am-2.30pm; Tuesday,Thursday and Friday 8am-2pm and 5-8pm.

There is also a duty rota for pharmacies so that at least one in the vicinity is open on Saturday and Sunday. Usually a note on the door of the pharmacy details the duty chemist.

The opening hours for pharmacies are fairly typical of the opening hours in small towns and villages. They argue, with some justification, everybody wants to sleep in the afternoon and nobody wants to shop.

In tourist areas, shopping hours are much more relaxed. Tourist shops in particular are open all day long but supermarkets, butchers, bakers and the like tend to observe more restricted hours.

The *periptero*, the corner-stone of Greek society, is open all day long and from there you can buy anything from chocolate to ice creams, soap to postage stamps and road maps to matches.

Sports & Pastimes

Water Sports

Recent years have seen a big increase in the popularity of wind surfing. Many of the small bays and coves are ideally suited to this sport and boards can be hired in most holiday resorts. Lessons for beginners are generally available at rates which are still very reasonable.

Water-skiing is available at many of the larger resorts. Further information can be obtained from: Water Skiing Association, 32 Stournara Street, Athens ☎ 523 1875.

Scuba diving is subject to certain regulations in Greece. More information on this and on the best coastal regions for scuba diving can be obtained from the Greek National Tourist Office.

Tennis

There are public tennis courts in Patra. Better class hotels in tourist regions often have facilities for tennis.

Golf

This is not a sport with a big following in Greece. The country boasts a total of four golf courses, one is at Glyfada just 12km (7 miles) from Athens but there are none in the Peloponnese.

Walking and Mountain Climbing

In a mountainous country like Greece riddled with old donkey trails there are abundant opportunities for walking. Unfortunately, there are no guide books describing short rambles or day hikes, although there are a number of such walks described in these pages. Long distance walkers have the opportunity to try the E4 European Rambler Trail which winds down through Greece from north of Florina to Githion in the southern Peloponnese. Further information outlining the route is available from the EOT and from the Hellenic Alpine Club, 7 Karageorgi Servias St, Athens ☎ 3234555. The HAC also supplies information, magazines, maps and guide books relating to mountain climbing and trekking in Greece.

Skiing

Facilities for skiing are on the increase in Greece. The season starts around mid-December and continues until the end of April. All the skiing resorts are equipped with ski lifts and have accommodation facilities. There are just two in this area.

Helmos Ski Centre, Peloponnese ☎ 0692 22174/22661
Menalo Ski Centre, Peloponnese ☎ 071232243

Telephone Services

Certain public telephone boxes, those marked with an orange strip at the top and usually with the word 'international,' can be used for long distance and international calls. They take only low value coins which means that conversation is constantly interrupted by a bleeping tone, a reminder to feed more money; not very convenient. Many *periptera*, the small kiosks which sell just about everything, have metered phones for public use. Some, but not all, will allow their use for international calls. These are useful in quiet locations but in a busy thoroughfare you have to compete with all the noise and bustle. The rate per call unit is not advertised so you will need to ask and the meter is often not displayed so you must rely on the vendors word for the number of units used.

Hotels have telephones for use by residents, mostly in the rooms but sometimes at reception. They charge a much higher rate per unit so ascertain the hotel rate and compare it with the rate at the Telecomunications office (OTE).

The cheapest and most convenient place to make telephone calls is from the Telecommunications office (OTE). This is normally part of or adjoining a main Post Office. If you are not sure where, look for a building with a large telecommunications dish and aerials on top, and head for that. Inside the OTE there are a number of telephone booths, mostly all international, but some still have a few dedicated to local calls. Choose a booth and note the number on the door. The call meter is set on the wall above the telephone and this should be set to zero. If not attract the attention of the counter clerk who will reset it. Only when it is on zero can you actually make a call. The ringing tone for an international call will be unfamiliar and depends on the destination country. An engaged tone is mostly a series of rapid bleeps. Throughout the call you can see the meter which usually displays the charge directly in *drachmas*. When the call is finished declare your booth number at the counter and pay.

International dialling codes from Greece are as follows: UK & Northern Ireland 0044: USA & Canada 001: Australia 0061: New Zealand: 0064. The internal code for Athens is 01.

Tipping

There are no hard or fast rules on tipping and certainly no fixed percentages. Restaurants and tavernas automatically include a service charge so there is no need to tip, but most Greeks pick the notes from their change leaving the small coins. If you intend to use a taverna regularly throughout your stay, a small tip will help to ensure continued good service. Taxi drivers do not normally get a tip from locals but they expect it from tourists. A tip would certainly be expected if they had been helpful in finding a restaurant or hotel for you. During Christmas and New Year and the whole of the Easter fortnight they are legally allowed to add a fixed tip to the bill. Hotel charges also include service and it is not usual to tip here but the porter and chamber maid are normally rewarded. Otherwise it is entirely discretionary.

Travel

The majority of visitors arrive by air, but travelling by road or rail is a distinct possibility for those starting out from European destinations.

By Air

Olympic Airways operates scheduled flights from Athens to many cities in western Europe and to destinations beyond including New York in the USA, Toronto and Montreal in Canada and Melbourne and Sydney in Australia. Foreign national carriers also operate services into Greece by reciprocal arrangements.

Charter flights offer much cheaper fares and there are many from Europe to Athens all year round. In season there are also flights to the Peloponnese, to Kalamata in the south and to the island of Zante, just off the west coast, which is well connected to Kilini on the mainland by an hourly ferry service.

Athens airport has two terminals. The West Terminal which handles Olympic Airways flights exclusively, both internal and international, and the East Terminal which handles international flights by all other carriers. Although these two terminals lie in different parts of the same complex, it is a lengthy journey around the perimeter to change from one to the other. The connecting bus service is of limited frequency out of the main season and taxis cope with the bulk of passenger transfers. Check the current taxi fare into Athens or between air terminals at the information desk on arrival. If faced with an ongoing internal flight, using Olympic Airways avoids the inconvenience of changing terminals. Both terminals have a frequent express bus service to Athens centre and regular airline buses connect with the Olympic and British Airways offices in Syntagma Square.

Internal flights are relatively inexpensive but, with the Peloponnese within easy motoring distance from Athens, only Kalamata in the south has a regular daily connection. Detailed flight information and bookings for any internal flight can be made in the country of departure by contacting Olympic Airways or national airlines with reciprocal arrangements or from leading travel agents. Domestic lines, especially on tourist routes, are well used throughout the holiday season so it pays to book in advance. The main ticket offices for Olympic Airways in Athens are located at:

Olympic Airways
6 Othonos Street
Syntagma Square
☎ 929 2555 (International)
  929 24444 (Domestic)

96 Syngrou Avenue
117 41 Athens
☎ 929 2251/4

By Rail

Rail fares to Greece are usually more expensive than charter flights, except if you are under 26 and can benefit from youth fares. Generally, you need to be young to withstand the rigours of the journey although it can be a lot more fun if you adopt the adage that it is better to travel than to arrive, and break the journey in various countries en route.

British Rail's InterRail pass, available to anyone living in Europe, allows one month's free travel on all railways in Europe. There is a proviso that you pay half the price of travel in the country of issue. The holder is entitled to reduced ferry fares on Channel crossings and on certain ferries between Italy and Greece.

Also of benefit to those under 26 are the Euro train or Transalpino tickets which, although costing more than the InterRail pass, allow for a stay of up to 2 months and include all ferry crossings. One-way tickets are also available at just over half the cost. Further information can be obtained from:

British Rail European Travel
Centre
Victoria Station
London SW1
☎ 071 834 9656

Transalpino
71-75 Buckingham Palace
Road
London SW1
☎ 071 834 9656

USIT/Eurotrain
London Student Travel
52 Grosvenor Gardens
London SW1
☎ 071 730 3402

By Road

The usual route from western Europe involves driving down through former Yugoslavia via Ljubljana, Zagreb, Belgrade and Skopje. Even with hard driving and only brief overnight stops, this requires a minimum of 4 days from England. At the moment, the unrest in this region provides the most compelling reason to seek an alternative way. Even when peace returns, it would be wise to await good reports before attempting this route.

Fortunately, there is a very attractive alternative which can also save a lot of driving. Head for Italy and use one of a number of car ferry services to Greece. Regular services operate all year round from a number of Adriatic ports. Listing from north to south, these include:-

Venice: does not figure prominently in timetables but the ferry boat *Marco Polo* provides a weekly service to Patra (Peloponnese).

Ancona: two/six sailings daily to Greece. Most call in at Corfu (about 26 hours) and Igoumenitsa (28 hours) on the way to Patra (36 hours) but there are also express services to Patra.

Bari: not a heavy timetable but there are daily sailings via Corfu (11 hours), Igoumenitsa (13 hours) to Patra (21 hours).

Brindisi: as many as eight sailings daily, mostly via Corfu (9 hours), Igoumenitsa (11 hours) to Patra (19 hours) and at least one express daily direct to Patra.

All the above listings run between Italy and Patra in the Peloponnese but, if you are looking for the experience of sailing through the Corinth canal to Piraeus (for Athens), there are not too many opportunities. The most famous name on this route is the *Orient Express* which sails from Venice to Istanbul although this is a cruise ship rather than a ferry boat. There is one genuine car ferry, the *Ariadne* which plies the route between Ancona in Italy and Kusadasi in Turkey via Piraeus. A number of the ferry companies operating these lines have agents in the UK. Their addresses are as follows:

Karageorgis Lines
36 King Street
London WC2E 8 JS
☎ 071 836 821

Mediterranean Passenger
 Services
9 Hanover Street
London W1R 8HF
☎ 071 499 0076

P&O European Ferries
Channel House
Channel View Road
Dover
Kent CT17 9TJ
☎ 0304 203388

Viamare Travel Ltd
33 Mapesbury Road
London NW2 4HT
☎ 081 452 8231

Travelling in Greece

Driving in Greece

Driving in Greece is on the right hand side of the road and overtaking on the left. Unless there are signs indicating otherwise, the speed limits are: built-up areas 50kph (31mph), outside built-up areas 80kph (50mph) and motorways 100kph (62mph).

Traffic moving along main roads outside towns has priority at intersections; in towns give way to traffic from the right. On approaching and on roundabouts, vehicles must give way to traffic coming from the right.

Unleaded fuel (*amolivthi venzini*) is increasingly available except in some remote country areas. The two grades of fuel (*venzini*) normally available are Apli (91/92) octane and Super (96/98) octane. Diesel is also widely available. Fuel is sold by the litre.

Driving in Athens city centre is subject to special restrictions. During the week, a ban on traffic is enforced according to car registration number plates where even numbers alternate on a daily basis with odd numbers. Restrictions apply 7am-8pm Monday to Thursday and 7am-3pm on Friday. Doctors and journalists are exempt from these restrictions at all times and foreign and hire cars, displaying a special sign, for the first 40 days.

Parking in cities is something of a problem and the best solution is not to try. Park in the suburbs and walk or bus into the centre. In Athens, parking in the Green Zone is restricted to parking meters only. Other regulations ban parking within 5m of an intersection, within 15m of a level crossing or bus stop and within 3m of a fire hydrant.

Illegal parking can result in a ticket which indicates the amount of the fine and where and when to pay it. The police are not empowered to collect on-the-spot fines. In Athens, illegal parking is dealt with differently. The car's number plates are removed and there is a heavy charge made to have them released.

With one of the worst accident rates in Europe, driving in Greece demands a cautious attitude from the onset. The discipline shown by the majority of drivers in western European countries, which brings order to traffic flow, is often missing from Greek drivers. Drive with your own safety in mind. Another major hazard is the state of the roads. Pot holes are a serious danger and can be encountered unexpectedly even on well surfaced roads. Some of the holes are large enough to cause damage to tyres and wheels. A line of rocks on the road guiding you towards the centre is the usual warning of edge subsidence and there will often be no other warning signs. Minor roads, which are well surfaced, may suddenly become unmetalled.

There is a 'motorway' linking Athens to Patra in the Peloponnese. It is a toll road and not of expected motorway standard as it is possible to encounter frequent and sudden changes in the number of lanes, for example, and there are roadside services.

Passenger cars, trailers, motor-cycles and side-cars can be cleared through Customs for use for four months (extendable) if the owner is the holder of a corresponding '*Carnet de Passage en Douane*' issued by the automobile and touring clubs of his country of origin. In the absence of such a document, motor vehicles are admitted temporarily without payment of import duty or tax by making an entry on the owner's passport whereupon a free use card is issued by the Customs.

Tourists from North America, Australia and South Africa have the right to use their automobiles for two years upon approval by the appropriate Customs Authority. Road taxes are paid for the second year.

Motorists from Britain, Germany, Belgium or Austria need only a valid driving licence from their home country, others require an International Driving Licence. These can be obtained from ELPA (address below) on production of a national driving licence and a passport or identification card. Again, passport-size photographs will be required. A Green Card International Motor Insurance Certificate is enough for drivers from Britain and most European countries. Visitors from USA, Canada, New Zealand and Australia will be required to buy local short term insurance on entry. The minimum age for driving a car in Greece is 18.

Greek law states that a car must carry a fire extinguisher, first aid kit and a warning triangle, but these are rarely found in hired vehicles.

The carrying of fuel in cans is forbidden as is the use of main beam headlights in towns and cities. Safety belts must be worn at all times and do not be dissuaded from this by the fact that many Greek motorists do not use them. There are days when the police crack down hard on offenders. These occasions are usually well advertised but the news may escape you, especially if you are on the move. The same warning applies to motor-cyclists. It is mandatory for driver and passenger to wear a crash helmet.

Information on all aspects of motoring can be obtained from the Automobile Association & Touring Club of Greece, ELPA, Athens Tower, 2-4, Messogion Street, 15 27 Athens ☎ 7791 615 to 629 & 7797 402 to 405

Car Hire

Greece is one of the more expensive countries for car hire and a better deal can be arranged by booking and paying in advance of departure. The minimum age for car hire is 21 but 25 for jeeps and minibuses. Clear with the hire company usage on ferries and trips out of Greece.

International car hire companies, such as Avis and Hertz are well represented in Greece. Also present are Europe Car, Budget and Eurodollar but with fewer hire stations. In Britain, companies like Holiday Autos offer very competitive rates. If you choose to use this option enquire which car hire company in Greece is involved. The quality of the back up service rather than the price may be the deciding factor ultimately, especially if you plan to tour widely. Wherever you are, it is comforting to feel that there is a branch of your car hire company not too far away in case of breakdown or similar problems. It is very likely that the car hire company will have membership of ELPA to cope with this situation, nevertheless, you can end up with a long drive or wait if there is a need to change the car. There are also local companies, InterRent and Just, for example, but choose carefully.

Third party insurance is compulsory under Greek law and this cost will be added to the hire charge. An additional optional insurance is collision damage waiver (CDW) and it is imperative to take it. This cannot be stressed too strongly. Should you be unfortunate enough to be involved in an accident without CDW insurance and the costs cannot be recovered from a third party then the consequences can be frightening. At best you may be faced with a huge repair bill, at worst you could end up in jail until it is fully paid.

Tyres and damage to the underside of the car are mostly excluded from the insurance cover. Take time when you are accepting the car to inspect the tyres and, if not fully satisfied, do not accept the vehicle. It is worth checking that lights and indicators are fully operational. Before driving away, make sure you have the agent's telephone number and a complete list of offices throughout the country.

Motor Cycles

Above comments on insurance apply also to hiring a motor-cycle or moped. There is a problem over crash helmets too. The law says very clearly that these must be worn but the chances that you will be able to hire them along with the bike are slim to nil. It is an unhappy situation which only compounds the personal dangers to motor-cyclists in a country which has a very high accident rate. If you intend to hire a motor-cycle, it is worth checking the fine print in the medical section of the holiday insurance taken out in your home country. Such is the concern over motor-cycle accidents that some companies are specifically excluding injuries arising this way.

Road Signs

Fortunately, international road signs are used throughout the country but there may be occasions when you encounter temporary signs written in Greek. Here are a few examples:

ΑΛΤ	Stop
ΕΛΑΤΤΩΣΑΤΕΤΑΧΥΤΗΤΑΝ	Reduce Speed
ΕΡΓΑ ΕΠΙ ΤΗΣ ΟΔΟΥ	Road Works In Progress
ΑΝΩΜΑΑΙΑ ΟΔΟΣΤΡΩΜΑΤΟΣ	Bad Road Surface
ΑΠΑΓΟΡΕΥΕΤΑΙ ΤΟ ΠΡΟΣΠΕΡΑΣΜΑ	No Overtaking
ΤΕΛΟΣ ΑΠΗΓΟΡΕΥΜΕΝΗΣ ΖΩΝΗΣ	End Of No-Overtaking
ΠΑΡΑΚΑΜΠΤΗΡΙΟΣ	Diversion
ΜΟΝΟΔΡΟΜΟΣ	One-Way Traffic
ΠΟΡΕΙΑ ΥΠΟΧΡΕΩΤΙΚΗ ΔΕΞΙΑ	Keep Right
ΑΠΑΓΟΡΕΥΕΤΑΙ Η ΣΤΑΘΜΕΥΣΙΣ	No Parking
ΑΔΙΕΞΟΔΟΣ	No Through Road

Accidents and Legal Advice

In the event of an accident involving personal injury or damage to property, both the law and your insurance require that it is reported to the police. To do this, dial 100 in most big cities or contact the Tourist Police by dialling 171 and ask their advice.

ELPA offer free legal advice concerning Greek legislation on car accidents and insurance.

Breakdowns

It is a legal requirement to place a warning triangle 100m behind the car. Next step is to dial 104 to obtain the road assistance service of ELPA (address on p155). This is available in and around all large towns in Greece.

ELPA has reciprocal arrangements with European motoring organisations, like the British AA and RAC, for road assistance, either a light repair on the spot or a tow to the nearest garage. Car hire firms are mostly members of ELPA but some have alternative arrangements for repair and assistance.

By Rail

The rail network in Greece is operated by the state-owned Hellenic Railways Organisation (OSE). Diesel trains run on narrow gauge lines in the Peloponnese and on standard gauge lines in the rest of Greece. This means that Athens has two stations which are located almost side by side. Larissis station provides services to Northern Greece and the international connections while Peloponnisos station serves the Peloponnese lines.

Most travellers book seats in advance and it pays to do so unless you prefer to travel standing in the corridor. Two classes are available and for long distance journeys, it is well worth considering first class if only for the extra space and additional comfort. First class costs around 50 per cent more than second class. There are no sleeper services but most long distance trains do have restaurant cars. Do not expect a fast journey on any line. Generally buses are quicker, even when lunch stops are included in the reckoning.

Tourist Information Centres

The head office is in central Athens: Greek National Tourist Office, 2 Amerikis Street, Athens ☎ 322 31 11 but this only deals with administration matters. Information for the public is supplied from two locations in nearby Syntagma Square. There are information desks at East (International) Airport and many frontier posts including Evzoni and Niki (which may be used entering from the former Yugoslavia), and the sea ports of Piraeus, Igoumenitsa and Patra.

The National Tourism Organisation of Greece, known as EOT within Greece, distributes attractively produced leaflets on all locations in Greece which include maps of the main towns and ancient sites. New stocks of up-to-date leaflets arrive in about March/April which is the best time to apply; by mid season demand often exceeds supply.

NTOG addresses around the world include:

UK and Ireland
4 Conduit Street
London W1R ODJ
☎ 071 734 599

Australia and New Zealand
51-57 Pitt Street
Sydney, NSW 2000
☎ 241 16 63

USA
645 Fifth Avenue
Olympic Tower (5th Floor)

New York NY10022
☎ 421 57777

168 North Michigan
Avenue
Chicago
Illinois 60601
☎ 728 1084

611 West 6th Street
Suite 2198 Los Angeles
California 90017
☎ 626 696

Travel Information

Foreign airline ☎ 96991
East airport ☎ 969 9466
Rail ☎ 524 0601
Road ☎ 512 4910
Sea ☎ 417 2657

Useful And Emergency Telephone Numbers

Doctors on call ☎ 105
Ambulance ☎ 166
Hospitals on duty ☎ 106
Pharmacies open ☎ 107
Aliens Police ☎ 770 5711
Coast Guard Emergency Patrol ☎ 108
Police ☎ 100
Port Authorities ☎ 103
Automobile Association ☎ 104
Automobile Association & Tourist Information ☎ 174
Information/International calls ☎ 169
Telephone information ☎ 134
Telephone Numbers in Greece ☎ 132
Telephone Numbers in Athens ☎ 131
Internal telephone information ☎ 162
International telegrams ☎ 165
Domestic telegrams ☎ 155

INDEX

Pages in **bold** type indicate maps